T0098695

the POWER *of* SETBACKS

the POWER *of* SETBACKS

How to Turn Your Mess Into
Your Success at Any Age

KAREN & DENNIS STEMMLE

New York

the POWER *of* SETBACKS

How to Turn Your Mess Into Your Success at Any Age

© 2017 Karen & Dennis Stemmle.

All rights reserved. No portion of this book may be reproduced, stored in a retrieval system, or transmitted in any form or by any means—electronic, mechanical, photocopy, recording, scanning, or other—except for brief quotations in critical reviews or articles, without the prior written permission of the publisher.

Published in New York, New York, by Morgan James Publishing. Morgan James and The Entrepreneurial Publisher are trademarks of Morgan James, LLC.
www.MorganJamesPublishing.com

The Morgan James Speakers Group can bring authors to your live event. For more information or to book an event visit The Morgan James Speakers Group at www.TheMorganJamesSpeakersGroup.com.

Shelfie

A free eBook edition is available with the purchase of this print book.

CLEARLY PRINT YOUR NAME ABOVE IN UPPER CASE

Instructions to claim your free eBook edition:
1. Download the Shelfie app for Android or iOS
2. Write your name in **UPPER CASE** above
3. Use the Shelfie app to submit a photo
4. Download your eBook to any device

ISBN 978-1-63047-880-3 paperback
ISBN 978-1-63047-881-0 eBook
ISBN 978-1-63047-882-7 hardcover
Library of Congress Control Number:
2015919188

Cover Design by:
Rachel Lopez
www.r2cdesign.com

Interior Design by:
Bonnie Bushman
The Whole Caboodle Graphic Design

In an effort to support local communities and raise awareness and funds, Morgan James Publishing donates a percentage of all book sales for the life of each book to Habitat for Humanity Peninsula and Greater Williamsburg.

Get involved today, visit
www.MorganJamesBuilds.com

Habitat for Humanity®
Peninsula and
Greater Williamsburg
Building Partner

TABLE OF CONTENTS

ACKNOWLEDGMENTS

Writing this book was far from an individual project, but the reality is if you want it to be read by thousands or hopefully millions of people it takes an entire team.

We would like to thank our son, Bradley, we love you very much and are so proud of you. We would like to thank our parents for all their years of love and support.

We also would like to thank: Karen's surgeon Doctor Gina Compagnoni who not only performed my surgery, but compassionately broke the "Big C" news to us. Doctor Manish Sawlani our personal physician who was with us every step of the way. Doctor Thomas Weyburn who gave Karen much more than support and care. The entire team at North Shore Oncology Group who administered my weekly chemo treatments and provided continual checkups during the recovery process. The amazing doctors, nurses, and staff at Good shepherd hospital in Barrington, Illinois.

We also would like to thank the team at Blue Cross Blue Shield of Illinois for taking care of our medical claims stress free. When you are fighting cancer, you don't need to be fighting your insurance company as well. .

To the entire Willow Creek Church Community especially the *Moms of Teens* group for their ongoing support and great homemade meals.

To Joel Comm for believing in our story and all your mentorship with this project. To Justin Spizman for helping architecting this book and continuingly challenging us to give more.

Another big thank-you goes to the entire team at Morgan James Publishing and Publisher David Hancock, for believing in our story and putting so much time and energy into this project.

Finally, we are thankful to all our friends and family. Without you, we would have never had the opportunity to share our message.

PREFACE

Dear Reader,

For us, it started as a way to cope. A way to wake up each and every day and have something to look forward to. It wasn't easy when Karen was diagnosed with cancer. It quickly felt as if we were drowning. But we knew we had no choice but to move forward and make lemonade out of our newest batch of lemons. There were days when Karen couldn't get out of bed; where her illness was overwhelming, and we simply had to deal. But then there were those days when she had the energy to leave the house. At first, we didn't know what to do. It had to be low stress and low impact. But it also had to put a smile on her face, and allow us some quiet and relaxation in a world filled with noise. So it didn't surprise either of us when Karen suggested we go for a drive on one of the "good days." And so we did.

By chance there was an estate sale in an upscale neighborhood around the corner. So we decided to go have a look. The process of wandering from room to room, discovering pieces of history and items that brought us back to our childhood, distracted us from the day-to-day challenges we were facing. In fact, for the first time we forgot about the cancer, even if just for a few hours. We were immediately hooked and every chance we got we would escape into this new world of adventure and discovery. The experience brought our whole family together, and allowed us to teach our son about our own childhood and family history, while creating new memories for us. We were able to teach him about our nation's history, about business, and about human interaction and spirit.

As you can imagine, we accumulated quite a lot of treasures during Karen's treatment and recovery. Going through cancer, you learn to appreciate living in the moment and the value of enjoying a laugh, a simple smile, or a big hug from your spouse or son. You are not thinking about your mortgage payment or other daily expenses that seem to consume so much of your thoughts during the course of your normal everyday life. When you face the potential of death at a relatively early age, you gain an unbelievable sense of clarity about the things that truly matter.

The Power of Setbacks is an inspirational journey highlighting our family's struggle with cancer and how it unexpectedly led to an amazing new life. It's all about the intersection of life and work, connecting with family, and redefining what really matters the most in life. The book is filled with practical advice and insights on overcoming challenges, achieving your dreams, and creating your own successful online business.

As time progressed and Karen's treatment was finally complete, she started the long recovery process. A process you just are not fully prepared for. It proved to be too much of a challenge for Karen to return to work in a full-time capacity. Mentally, she wanted to get back to a normal life as soon as possible, but her body was not ready to respond. As she focused on the new fight, her recovery, I suggested she start selling some of those acquired treasures, if for no other reason, than to clear out the house. Before we knew it, we were buying wholesale and surplus lots and providing retailers with inventory liquidation services.

Our distraction from cancer unexpectedly turned into a full-time business. In July of 2014, we left the Chicago area and moved to the Myrtle Beach, SC area to fully embrace the *Resale Millionaire* lifestyle. We were given lemons, and we opened up a lemonade stand. We have always lived by the mantra that life is not what happens to you, but what you do with it. And this experience was no different. This is how our journey through cancer has brought us to where we are now. We want to give you the freedom to take control and face your fears. We want to show you how to have faith and follow your dreams, branch out of your comfort zone, and live a fuller life.

A *Resale Millionaire* is anyone who lives their life in pursuit of their own passions and dreams. They are not focused on the size of their bank account, but instead on the size of their lives. With this book, our goal is to not only help create an environment and culture that connects you to what matters the most, but also show you the lemons that yield the most juice, as well as the ones that will rot and eat up your profits. One man's lemons are another man's treasure.

We have gone from working a conventional workweek and living a traditional life to facing the unthinkable. Our out of the box thinking, business success, and entrepreneurial knowledge, both on and offline, enabled us to grow from idea to concept, and eventually to success. Now we're living the lifestyle we wanted with more time for family and friends. We have experienced the lows of life and faced them straight on and came out stronger for it. Yes we have even made a few mistakes and will steer you away from them in the direction of success. This is not just a concept, but also our reality. Our efforts have paid off and we have made it fun and easy for you to make money online.

When you face the potential death of your soul mate, somehow the money you made fades to the background. No matter how many garage sales we visited, time was never for sale. We were just focused on beating the disease and surviving. Armed with the time to reflect, we developed a new perspective and we set out to make major changes in our lives. We knew we needed to focus on what was really important to us—family and friends, controlling our time, our income, and inspiring and coaching others to live the life they deserve.

The information in this book is not academic theory or untested hypothesis; it comes directly from our time in the trenches. We have learned that the traditional measure of success is really a trap and an illusion; so often we spend our lives making a living, and we forget to just live. I have spent time digging ditches and in the company of billionaires. I have seen the world from many different perspectives and I can tell you without question that a focus on the material things in this world will not bring you the happiness you desire. A company I co-founded was sold to a publicly traded firm for seven figures. I always felt I was born with entrepreneurial blood running through my veins. But applying that same "go get it" attitude to life was certainly a learned trait.

This book is not about getting rich in four hours a week or becoming a millionaire in just one year. We aren't saying it can't happen, we are just saying that our measuring sticks are higher than just financial ones. It is all about finding that intersection between work and life that allows you to truly live. We will entertain, educate, inspire, and encourage you to reflect on what really matters the most. Along the way, we will provide a practical guide you can use to make a few hundred to a few thousand of dollars a month while simultaneously increasing the quality of your lives. Money that can be used to take that epic vacation, help with the mortgage or credit card bills, fund that college education, or just supplement your retirement. Applying these principles consistently over time will help you to live your entrepreneurial dreams.

If we can, then you can! We'll show you a new way to see the world around you. Reconnect with your history and share it with others. Teach life lessons from facing fears, managing money, budgeting, negotiating, and learning many other fundamental business principles. Who doesn't like a good treasure hunt? It gives you a way to relate to both the young and old, while getting to know your community and making new connections or rekindling old ones. *The Power of Setbacks* will give you the opportunity to change your perspective on things and see a new life and purpose.

This book will give you all you need to know to build your business and improve your life. Looking back, we learned it is the things you can't buy that truly had the most value: the time, the love, the friendship, and the welcomed distraction.

We are excited to take you on this journey.

Karen and Dennis Stemmle

Chapter 1

THE ADVENTURE:
From Fear to Faith

*I*t was a sunny summer afternoon in Barrington Hills, Illinois when we set out for a quick drive through horse country. There is something about watching a group of horses running in the open pastures that just seems to relax me. I enjoy watching the foils run, jump and play alongside their moms. To me, the scene represents a sort of carefree, fun freedom for which we all seem to long. Along the way, our family came across an estate sale sign and on a whim we decided to go check it out. Little did we realize at the time that what we thought was an insignificant and random detour would set into place an unlikely chain of events, which would ultimately culminate in the amazing experiences that lead to writing this book.

As we pulled up the winding driveway to the house, we immediately noticed an older Mercedes about 100 yards from the entrance to the home. In its window, there was a large handwritten sign that said "For Sale." Of course, my husband Dennis had to immediately pull over to check out the available vehicle. After inquiring, we learned that the lady's husband had recently passed away and she was moving to Florida to be closer to her grandchildren. Since we had lived in numerous cities in Florida, we struck up a very nice conversation about Florida and how much we missed the beaches and warmer climate.

After about 10 minutes, we headed up to a beautiful split level home on a sloping lot with an English walk out basement. As we walked in the front door, my eyes were immediately drawn to a piece of artwork still hanging over the fireplace. The art depicted a picture of a lake along a hilly landscape. The scene triggered a flow of childhood memories that brought back a flood of emotions all at once. When I was a child, my entire family would head up to Lake San Antonio in California for a week of family fun and bonding. We would roast marshmallows, hike, boat, and play all day long on the beach. The picture in front of me transported me back to those cherished vacations. The feeling was so strong that I could not only close my eyes and see our camper lakeside, I could even smell the Kentucky Fried Chicken we would always pick up to eat on the first night by the campfire.

As I returned back to the moment, we realized we were blocking the entrance for the group of people coming into the home and decided to move into the living room to take a closer look at the painting. We spent a few minutes in front of that picture and I started telling Dennis about the stories from my childhood. Over half an hour flew by as we sat there talking. But it was in that half-hour that, for the first time, I had escaped the then current reality of my battle with cancer. The conversation was energizing and I was excited to walk through the house and see what else we might find. I really don't recall much else about the items in the home, but the feelings I felt that day would not leave my thoughts for weeks to come. So much so that I was excited to head to any estate or garage sale I could find. That hour or so had changed everything for me, as I had reverted back in time and relived warm yet dormant memories. And it was through that experience and that moment that I knew I could never give up the fight, as I knew I had way too many memories yet to create with my own family. It was that picture at that house at that estate sale that gave me all I needed to remain motivated and inspired to do all I could to win my battle against cancer.

Over the coming weeks and months, we became regulars at garage sales, yard sales, bazaar sales, flea markets, antique malls, and anywhere else we might find treasures from the past. We started to purchase things that brought back positive memories from our past or elicited some meaningful emotions from within. We also started to purchase items we just found to be unique or even represented just a plain old good deal. But I really knew we were in trouble when Dennis muttered in disbelief that they were asking only $1 for a bunch of all-weather floor mats. To my surprise, he sold them three days later for $78.00. I wasn't the only who caught the bug: He was hooked as well.

On only our second estate sale visit, we came across a group of pictures and posters in a room that were each marked for $3.00 a piece. As we looked through the pile we noticed a couple of the posters were actually signed. One in particular was a Jazz festival poster from 1997 that was signed by B.B King and eleven or twelve other artists. The poster turned out to be worth $1,500, and if our first estate sale did not have us hooked, this trip sealed the deal for us. We quickly learned that for most people who owned the piles of treasures, they just wanted it to be moved, and were willing to almost give it away. The most efficient way for them to move these items out was to group them into logical bundles and mark them for sale. What had started as a simple escape, had now turned into a weekly excursion and treasure hunt that the whole family would look forward to; a treasure hunt that would provide us life lessons while creating new memories, and lead us on a completely new direction in life.

The Journey: How Garage Sales Kept Us Going

It was May 10, 2011, and I was in the kitchen making breakfast. When I brushed against my left breast, I paused and thought it was weird it did not feel sore or painful. Upon investigation, I found a solid lump that I could circle with my fingers, and I quickly knew I was in trouble. Waiting for the doctor's office to open proved to be the most challenging and longest hour of my life. But when I called, the nurse agreed to squeeze me in and suggested I hop in the car. When I arrived at the office and finished filling out the regular paperwork, I was ushered in to meet with my doctor. It didn't take her long to confirm that there was a 2 CM lump within my breast. She wrote me a script to get a mammogram and gave me the card for a surgeon in case one would be needed. I called the hospital right away to get the mammogram scheduled and they indicated they could fit me in within thirty minutes. During the mammogram, the lump was clear as day and its image was haunting. I knew this would not be good news.

They told me that a follow-up ultra-sound was necessary, and the results showed a semi-solid lump and a suspicious lymph node. The radiologist came in and told me these needed to be biopsied. It was all sort of surreal and I was not sure how to process it all. My treating physician called me the next day and told me to schedule a meeting with the surgeon.

On Tuesday May 17, 2011, around 2:30 pm., I was at the surgeon's office waiting to see the doctor. She entered the room in which I was sitting, and quickly told me that the pathologist confirmed it was a cancerous lump. After bringing Dennis into the room, he asked how things were going; to this point, he didn't really have any reason to think my worst fears were a reality. As he entered the room, I glanced in his direction and offered him the news. I told him it was cancer while extending my fist to do a fist bump like we always did. He bumped my fist with his, and in that very awkward and goofy moment, we both knew that we would not let this beat us.

Leading to that day, I kept on telling Dennis he did not need to go with me to the doctor. I guess I was just minimizing and didn't want him to worry. But it was in his nature to be there for me and (like most of the time) he didn't listen. He insisted on coming along. In hindsight, I am so glad he was there. Once I received the diagnosis, I couldn't focus and certainly was unable to process the dumping ground of information that came next. While Dennis intently listened, I was in a helpless fog, unable to focus and caught in a circle of pure fear.

Fast forward a few days, and I would have surgery to remove the cancerous area. The lump turned out to be T2N2 stage 11 triple negative invasive ductile cancer. Luckily, it had worked its way to just one lymph node. In an abundance of caution, they removed a total of four, but only one showed signs of cancer. The tumor was 3 cm and the margins were clear. She told us the triple negative means the systemic treatment the medical oncologist would want to go with would be chemo and a local treatment of radiation. So as we knew it, the next step in my battle would be the dreaded chemo followed by radiation.

Recovery would turn out to be a bigger ordeal and a much longer process than any of us anticipated. For me, it started the day after surgery and still continues through the writing of this book. When I returned home from surgery, I took off the tube top they wrapped around me. It was a Velcro pink wrap with flowers. I took a gander in the mirror to see what I would find, and unexpectedly saw the initials G.C., presumably standing for the name of my surgeon. She must have thought she did such a good job that she would autograph her work. I have to say I did not expect to see that!

After surgery, the pain began to subside each day, and eventually I was strong enough to begin my chemo and the battle ahead.

I started my chemo on June 30th, 2011, and would finish my radiation treatments in December of 2011. I went for chemo treatments every two weeks, and tried my best to remain positive. I had very long, thick curly hair and having it come out bit by bit would be a mess. So in anticipation of what was to come, I took the proactive approach and had a shaving party with some of my friends. It was less of a party since I was the only one getting shaved.

The chemo process was both physically and mentally draining on my body. Luckily, my family, friends, and employer were great through the entire process. One thing I had stuck in my mind from the beginning was that I was not going to let the cancer define me. I was not going to give into being a victim of cancer. I was committed to continuing to work my full time job and only taking a small amount of time off. I wanted to go to my treatments by myself, and I was going to work to be there for the other people who had cancer and didn't have the support system I had. I felt the need to keep strong and not give into the cancer. I was initially reluctant to accept help, as I did not want to be seen as weak, but I soon realized that no one could do it alone, and so I gradually began to accept the help when it was offered.

Cancer is really as much of a battle fought within your mind, as it is one fought inside of your body. Cancer diminishes your energy level to point that you rarely have the energy to do most of what you love. The distractions and the coping mechanisms are scarce because you often don't have the necessary energy to even leave the house. But when we walked into that estate sale, I found myself completed distracted and engulfed in the process of going through the assortment of items and looking for that hidden gem or special treasure that triggered a memory. I was amazed at how items transformed me back to my childhood, reminded me of a special time or event, and just made me smile or laugh. At the time, I had no idea how lucky we were to have stumbled upon such an amazing sale. I often wonder what would have happened if we had not stumbled upon that sale! Call it luck or divine intervention, but it was that initial garage sale that opened the door to an opportunity to find meaning and purpose and joy during my difficult battle with cancer.

In the weeks and months that followed, Dennis and I visited estate sales, flea markets, antique malls, moving sales, and garage sales. Even when I was down and out from radiation, I could always muster up just enough energy to find a good sale. I can tell you the experience and bargain priced replacement for retail therapy was not just a distraction for me, but also for the whole family. It gave us something to talk about other than the "Big C." Dennis and our son Bradley found it was a great way to spend quality family time together. Bradley got a kick out of seeing items that predated the iPhone and Internet. For those of you with teenagers, you know just how hard it can be to find those things that cross generations and bring a family together. Bradley and Dennis loved to see the look on my face when they would bring me an item they knew I would like. The whole family began to look forward to the sales.

Even though it was not the "normal" we were used to, we found a new way to live. Garage sales replaced the difficult conversations we had about treatment. Talks about scheduling radiation were traded in for conversations about the next big sale. And my sadness was pushed out by the happiness I experienced as I watched my family come together and bond over these outings. Win, lose, or draw, we were living a new type of dream, which had replaced an unexpected nightmare.

As time progressed and the growing number of purchases filled our house, necessity became the mother of invention. Or was it an intervention? We agreed I had to start selling the items. It was fun to see how I could turn someone's unwanted goods into money. And I got pretty good at it. I was not only listing the items we had accumulated, I was making a profit too. It was addicting to hear the cash register sound my phone made when something sold on Ebay. Little did I know I was using cancer to fuel an entirely new hobby and love within my life. Talk about a silver lining.

The Gift of Garage Sales

Think about the last time your child put away his electronics and begged you to go for a ride around town to see if there were any garage sales. For us, that became the norm. Our son, Bradley, loved joining us on our journey. He has proved to have a good eye and different perspective on the entire process. He is also improving his negotiation skills, budgeting abilities, and business acumen. In fact, we watch him ask questions, research items, and learn an enormous amount about the history of many of the items we purchase and even those we don't. We get to spend time together learning about our history.

Cancer affected all of us in different ways. While I was suffering the physical issues of the illness, Bradley and Dennis had a much more emotional aspect to it. But these sales diverted their stress and sadness and replaced them with a smile and a grin. We cherished our time together.

It is easy to get caught in the sadness and stress of a scenario as difficult as cancer. It is very easy to focus on the negatives and find yourself caught in an onslaught of negative thoughts. Visiting garage sales is one way we lived in the here and now, while looking to the past with joy and the future with hope. As we treasure hunted through the items, we had a common goal and focus that was a welcome distraction from the cancer.

Through our experience, we came to realize that the item at which we were looking was not nearly as important as the people in our lives, and the journey we were on together as a family. I would not give up anything for the laughter, smiles and adventures we would find along the way in search of the next garage sale. It turns out that garage sales are really a neat way to find items, and to meet people as well. One morning we were following garage sale signs, not knowing where the next turn would be. It occurred to me that following these signs was much like living your life; you just don't know what awaits. When we arrived at this particular house, we noticed a custom license plate with our family name on it. We were quite surprised and excited, and as we spoke with the owners we discovered we were related. Living less than 20 minutes from us, some 1,000 miles from our nearest known relative, we had connected with a part of our family tree that had somehow been lost through time. We of course had to buy a few items at this sale, as they would serve as a reminder of the day we learned a little more about our family heritage.

The reality is that family bonding, education, and even finding some long lost relatives are just a few of the gifts garage sales gave to us. The same can be true for you. As you progress through this book, you'll find out a lot about the buying and selling of second-hand items. You will learn about how to locate the sales, how to negotiate at them, how to budget and plan for them, and how to sell your new purchases.

Taking a Look at the Bigger Picture

There are all kinds of items at a garage sale, and almost as many kinds of personalities. What makes one person see a treasure and another see clutter? What gives one person joy in selling and the other in buying? It is often difficult to say. But as we enter new chapters of our lives, we no longer have a need for many of the things that once played a role in our daily routines. Times change. And a diagnosis like cancer will really push you to take the time to assess what really matters.

Perspectives can be a funny thing. I recall the day I was washing my hair and it all came out in my hands. Dennis's response was sheer excitement because he knew the chemo was doing its job and killing the cancer. For me, it redefined the definition of a bad hair day. We all have things happen in our lives—moving mid school year, the death of a family member, or the loss of a job; but it is how we respond to these events that makes all the difference. Our reaction is what dictates our ultimate journey. At times, we have very little control over what is thrown our way. What we do have control over is our response to those inevitable challenges thrown at us.

Will you react or act with thought and purpose? We acted with positive actions and conviction, and decided that we were going to get through this obstacle. Seeing it for what it was and respecting the magnitude of it was our choice response. We were not going to get swallowed by the ordeal. We'd look at the course of action and take it one step at a time. I focused on one treatment at a time. I didn't get caught up with the notion of how I was going to do it again. I had to stay with each treatment to deal with the effects of the chemo, and the fatigue and discomfort of the radiation. No one knows how he or she is going to react when adversity hits. For me, I soon realized the nausea would not last forever and would pass and return and pass again. All I needed to do was hold on, knowing that time and the anti-nausea meds would be my friend. I knew I had to take care of myself before I could do anything for Dennis or Bradley. As I was dealing with the effects of the cancer treatment, I had to trust in my faith that our family would be fine.

It is not what happens to you, but what you do when life happens to you! I will always follow the sign to the next garage sale. I will take the next turn and remain excited to see what will come from the bends in the road.

But the question remains: What will you do to embrace the treasures that are around your next turn?

Opening the Garage Door

We are hooked on the chance to spend time together, hear amazing stories, meet new people, find great deals, and leave our troubles behind.

Garage sales allow us to get out of our head and see the beauty around us—namely our friends, family, and each other. What turned out to be an escape from my battle with cancer turned into a rather large collection of items that literally took over our house. During my leave of absence from work, we started to list these items on eBay and Amazon, as a way to reclaim our house. We were selling them and making a profit. We also had discovered a great way to teach our son negotiation techniques, money management, and social interaction skills. Not to mention one of life's great lessons—the law of "supply and demand."

It turned out that friends and family were interested in learning about how our weekend wanderings had turned into an online business. So we started to spend hours teaching others how to do what we were doing. We routinely had people ask us if we needed help or if we could come show them how they could do the same thing. We discovered that many people wanted to escape the 9 to 5 routine and take control of their own future, but just did not know how. Often, it is an unforeseen event that serves as the catalyst to fuel changes in your life.

We don't want you to have to go through cancer or some other life event before you take action to pursue your dreams. It does not have to be an all or nothing proposition to get started. The great thing about our book is that anyone who wants to make a little extra money, or who wants to significantly change their lives, can easily get started without taking significant risks.

What started out for us as an unfortunate diagnosis of cancer and a need to deal with what was going on as a family, transformed our lives and evolved into a successful business for all of us. We didn't expect it, and it surprises us each and every day. *Resale Millionaires* is all about creating the life you desire and living life to its fullest. We developed a model we will share with you that will allow you to not wait for the "Big C" to come knocking at your door for you to take control and step out of your comfort zone. We will show you how to start making money online whenever you are ready.

We will show you the way. We have walked these steps and will give you tips to make the right choices to get the most profits. We will tell you where to go, what to buy, and how to sell it to turn a profit. This book is your blueprint to follow in order for you to become a *Resale Millionaire*. The steps we outline turned our mess into our success—it is now your turn! The treasures are out there, and if you don't get them then who will? What are you going to do the next time you see that garage sale sign? It's your turn to create your own reality, achieve your dreams, and build a successful and non-traditional business.

Your journey starts now.

Chapter 2

LESSONS FROM
THE JOURNEY:

Turning Your Mess into Success

As Jack Gallo said on the popular television show *Just Shoot Me,* "Sometimes on the way to your dream, you get lost and discover a better one." For us, the journey started as a nightmare. And we weren't exactly sure if it would ever turn into a dream. But as we put one foot in front of the other, we discovered an opportunity we never could have imagined. That opportunity brought us happiness, quality time together, and a much-needed distraction from what seemed like an impossible situation.

There is an introspective commercial running that traces a young couple through a series of life's "never going to happen to them" moments. In the commercial, they never get married, never have kids, never move to the suburbs, never buy that minivan, and for what it is worth, never really accomplish any of the goals they set. Of course, each subsequent scene in the commercial shows them embracing their *never* from the scene just prior.

Sometimes, life feels a lot like that commercial. It has a way of just happening and before you know it, you miss many opportunities and the idea of *never* is now your current reality.

On our journey, we learned that success is just one dimension driving our happiness, but certainly not the most important one. In reality, the other and more significant dimension is fulfillment. You likely will not find fulfillment if you are constantly focused on making money or working harder. Time will inevitably pass you by, leaving you with little to show for it. To prevent that, it is essential to stop, reflect and ask different kinds of questions. Take the time to focus on figuring out what you really want.

What do you want your life to look like?

What is your true purpose and passion?

We learned that success really meant achieving a greater level of true fulfillment and leading a much more meaningful and happy life. We realized that success in its traditional form was just one of our lives' dimensions, but one that had taken center stage and had served as a driving force for too many of our decisions. We were so worried about succeeding that we were absolutely failing in the meantime.

Fulfillment is creating the sense that your life has meaning and internal peace and happiness. It is a feeling that you are moving in the right direction, you are pursuing those things that matter to you, and you feel like you are making a real difference in the world.

We learned that most people are driven to seek success, but if that success is unfulfilling, they still feel hollow inside once the journey is over. In reality, people are actually looking for fulfillment. Success is traditionally defined by external measures—how much money you earn, your job title, the car you drive, the neighborhood in which you live, and your position in the community. Once you obtain these trappings, you find yourself thinking: "Is this it? There must be more!"

Success in itself is a worthy pursuit; it is just that success is only one piece of the equation. We often mistakenly believe that by being successful, we will achieve happiness and fulfillment. But that couldn't be further from the truth. We discovered there is no exact correlation between success and feelings of happiness and fulfillment. They may come hand in hand, but then again, they may not.

If you want a real wake up call, go visit your local senior center or retirement home. Talk to those people about their regrets, and you will find they don't regret the things they have done as much as the things they never did. The common theme will be the regret from what they left on the table, not from what they actually ate. And quickly, you will find that hardly any of these people who have most of their time behind them will tell you that the happiest moments in their lives were defined by the things they owned or the money they made.

So, how can you make sure your "one day" actually arrives? How can you avoid the peril of achieving your goals, only to find yourself feeling empty and unsatisfied? How can you avoid that one big regret?

Tough questions to answer, right? Our collective goal is to help you avoid these difficult circumstances, and create what we call the "Life Vision Alignment Model." With a lot of thought, reflection, and effort, you can create your own roadmap to your own personal paradise. The "Life Vision Alignment Model" will help you find your way and ensure that your reality is one of which you are proud and fulfilled.

Fulfilled people draw little distinction between their work and their play, their labor and their leisure, their education and entertainment, and their mind, body, and spirit. They simply pursue their personal vision for their lives. The average person has no clear sense of his purpose, and that is exactly why he feels lost, stressed, empty, and just plain average.

Do you feel that way?

What is your life purpose?

Do you expect success and happiness? A life of fulfillment?

Are you stuck on the treadmill of vagueness?

Do you lack focus?

If so, let's take the time to evaluate why you feel that way and then analyze how we can make the necessary changes to ensure that feeling doesn't follow you around like a small rain cloud.

There are five areas where you have to be absolutely clear about your purpose if you are going to turn your mess into your success and your success into fulfillment:

1. Your Vision
2. Your Career
3. Your Health
4. Your Finances
5. Your Alignment

Your Vision

You are not going to create a clear and well-thought-out vision overnight. Envisioning your life's purpose and determining your life's course requires a substantial amount of time and reflection. You should work to develop a vision and then apply a significant amount of thought and planning to turn your vision into a practical plan. Your vision is developed from determining your dreams, passions, hobbies, hopes, and aspirations. Alignment with your values and ideals will help you to achieve success in living your life's vision. This alignment will help generate the energy and enthusiasm required to strengthen your commitment to pursuing all the possibilities your new vision holds. A simple way to get started is to ask yourself:

What do I want?

This question may sound deceivingly simple, but it's often the most difficult question to answer. Don't self-regulate here just because you believe writing a big goal or desire will be unattainable. Give yourself permission to explore all your potential dreams and desires.

Remember, this can and should be a slightly uncomfortable experience for you. You may think it is too late to dream about what you want out of life, but it's important to remind yourself that it is never too late to live the life of your dreams. A life of fulfillment does not typically happen by chance, but rather by design.

It's helpful to ask some thought provoking questions to help you discover the possibilities of what you want out of life. Consider every aspect of your life, personal and professional, tangible and intangible. Contemplate all the important areas like family and friends, career and success, health and quality of life, spiritual connection and personal growth, and our favorite, fun and enjoyment. Below are some tips to guide you in your journey:

- Remember to ask *why*? For example, you may list making $100,000 a year as a goal, but why do you really want the money? Remember, money is just paper. In reality, you actually may be seeking the things money buys: prestige, security, or simply self-enrichment.
- It is also useful to think about what you *don't* want. Don't disregard your experiences and life lessons already learned. If you know you do not like being stuck inside all day, use that knowledge as a compass to direct you toward your dreams.
- Ask friends and family what they think your ideal life would look like. Others will often consider ideas that you never thought possible. Inviting mentorship into your life can be a huge help along your journey.

- Make a list of things that you think would bring more joy and happiness into your life.
- Consider what issues or causes you care about, and then figure out how you can get involved.
- What relationships would you like to strengthen, add, or eliminate in your life? Start making the shifts one by one.
- What skills or qualities would you like to develop? Once you have a list, pick up a book or hop on the Internet to begin your educational journey.
- What are your talents? What's special about you? We all have unique selling points. Ask your friends what they respect about you the most.
- What would you like your legacy to be? Write it down and read it everyday before you leave the house.
- How would you spend your time if you never had to work again? Then spend some time each day doing it.

Once you have thoroughly reflected on these questions and written down the answers, you are primed to tackle the process of creating your own personal vision statement. Keep in mind that your personal vision statement can and will likely change over time. As you mature, it is likely the driving forces of your life will change and require adjustment. However, you will be amazed at how many items remain consistent over time, no matter your age or your development.

Your personal vision statement will serve as a guide for your life and provide you with the necessary direction to ensure that the choices you make stay aligned with your life's objectives. Your vision statement should project forward into time and present a picture, like a dream, of how things should eventually look. Usually, a vision statement works best as a story about the future, with your life as the key element in the story.

It can be as long or as short as you find practical. Your vision statement can include such items as reading, publishing books, sharing your knowledge with people, having a positive impact on your community, living a life of meaning, loving your significant other, valuing people, friends, and family relationships, being more present and engaged in your environment, traveling the world, creating financial security, improving your health and fitness, controlling your time, and much more. There are no limitations.

Steve Job's personal vision statement was "to innovate at the intersection of the humanities and technology."

Einstein's famous vision statement was "to know the mind of God." Enormous, but then again, he was Einstein.

Here are a few other vision statements from some famously high achievers:

"To have fun in [my] journey through life and learn from [my] mistakes." — Sir Richard Branson, Founder of the Virgin Group

"To serve as a leader, live a balanced life, and apply ethical principles to make a significant difference." — Denise Morrison, CEO of Campbell Soup Company

"To be a teacher. And to be known for inspiring my students to be more than they thought they could be." — Oprah Winfrey, Founder of OWN, the Oprah Winfrey Network

"To use my gifts of intelligence, charisma, and serial optimism to cultivate the self-worth and net-worth of women around the world." — Amanda Steinberg, founder of Dailyworth.com

Armed with your personal vision statement in hand, we can now dig into the key pillars of your life: your career, your health, and your finances.

Your Career: Job or Business

Perhaps one of the more difficult decisions we make in our lives is choosing a career. So much of our identity is tied to our career that it often becomes an integral part of who we are and how we are perceived. In fact, many of us would define our worth by our career. Meet someone for the first time and you are likely to hear, "So, What do you do?"

At some point in most of our lives we will wonder whether we should leave the corporate world behind and enter the exciting world of entrepreneurship. Many of the younger generation are questioning whether they even want to enter the corporate world at all. With the emergence of the Internet and cloud based hosting solutions, the cost to start a business has never been lower.

For most, starting a part-time business and allowing that business to gain traction and momentum while maintaining a full-time job is a sound and rational approach. This approach allows you to earn while you learn, and reinvest your earnings right back into your business. For others, you may simply consider a path to earning additional money each month while having fun with friends and family. That was where we began.

Whichever approach you take, there are a few trade-offs to consider. Based on our own experiences, we will try and provide you with an honest account of the lifestyle and the trade-offs. Let's start by looking at some of the more challenging aspects of owning your own business.

Where's My Weekend? Unlike a typical office job, there is no notion of a weekend when you own your own business. In fact, you will find most of the days start to blend together. You will find you run your errands on weekdays to avoid the masses on the weekend. You will likely realize you need to put in more hours than you thought necessary in order to accomplish your goals.

Where's My Paycheck? One of the biggest challenges in launching your own business is that your earnings are inherently unpredictable.

This is especially true if your business is brand new; however, chances are you'll have wide variability in your earnings in any given month.

When Do I Relax? In the beginning, you don't. When you own your own business, you'll stress out over everything, even the things that are beyond your control. Your livelihood depends on proper execution, so there can be no excuses. Every problem you encounter has your name on it and it is up to you to deal with it. If you are jumping in full-time and trying to establish your business from scratch, you can pretty much kiss any free-time or social life goodbye. You will want to ramp up as fast as possible, and focusing on your business becomes priority number one. That doesn't mean you have to be a slave to your business, but a new business is like a new puppy—it needs a ton of attention or it will likely tear your life apart.

But it's not all challenges.

The benefits of owning your own business vary widely, but the opportunity to create wealth, control your own time, make your own decisions, and directly impact results are among the benefits we love. We have found running our own business allows us to allocate our work across bigger time blocks. We do not have to get things done during traditional business hours. This gives us the flexibility to manage our time as we see fit. The other advantage is that we can hire people to help us out. Imagine trying to hire someone to do your regular job for you. It just wouldn't fly. "Hi, I am Chris. Dennis asked that I come to work in his place today. He is tired and overworked. Where is his desk?" Not a chance on that one.

With a regular corporate job, you never feel personally responsible for things that are beyond your control. For example, if you're an IT developer and your company's marketing team makes a critical mistake in positioning the product that you designed, you might be disappointed, but you probably wouldn't lose a ton of sleep over it. Not your problem.

Typical corporate politics are gone, but politics are replaced with having to raise the capital to execute on your plans. Many corporations can (and do) go years without making a profit; your small business will not have that luxury.

It's easy to forget that changing careers will affect your family too. Be certain that you and your loved ones understand the implications of starting a business. The risks you take for your business should be intentional and calculated, but at some point, you likely will have to just take a leap of faith.

To minimize the financial burden on your family, calculate your living costs every month, and make sure you have enough saved to survive at least 12 to 18 months without any income. Make sure you establish critical checkpoints to evaluate your progress along the way.

When launching a business, cash is king, so get rid of any unnecessary expenses and minimize your overhead in the beginning, and until you can track your likely monthly earnings.

With that in mind, here are five questions that might help determine if you have a business owner's mindset before you take that fateful leap:

1. Can you work independently?

Business owners know how to enjoy working independently. They take full ownership for creating and completing their own work tasks and schedules. They are very driven and hyper-focused. If you are thinking about starting a home-based business, there will be times when you'll be spending hours working alone, without social interaction with others. For some, that is worse than going back to their day job.

2. Are you goal orientated?

As a business owner you are now responsible for planning, budgeting, marketing, and overseeing the success of the business. Running a successful business requires you to formulate and implement a well thought-out business plan. You will have to develop a mission statement, an innovative vision for your company, short and long-term financial goals, and an effective market plan.

3. Can you multi-task?

Successful entrepreneurs are masters at creating focus among the daily chaos. They are experts at time management and multi-tasking. Self-discipline is a key factor to creating a successful business. A business owner must be consistent, but flexible. In order to be consistent, you must be self-directed and self-motivated to do those things that must be done, day in and day out, to keep your business moving forward. In the simplest words, it is about doing what you need to do even when you don't feel like doing it.

4. Can you budget and measure success?

If you decide to start a business, how do you intend to fund your business operations? If your plan is to use the cash flow from operations to fund your first year of operation, then you are destined for failure, or at least an enormous amount of unwelcomed risk. Have you taken any accounting or business classes, or even spoken to others that have gone down the same path before you? Do you know how to forecast, establish critical success measures, or monitor and evaluate your progress? If not, be sure to learn these essential tools before you take the leap.

5. Are you comfortable with no steady paycheck?

Business owners are responsible for their own pay, retirement plan, taxes, insurance, and much more. There will likely be times when you won't be able to draw a paycheck. Running your own business means taking risks and living with the financial uncertainty that often comes along with it.

Are you prepared to take the financial risks? Are you willing to live with the stress that often comes along with giving up a steady paycheck?

While the answers to these questions may seem daunting and overwhelming, most entrepreneurs believe that they are either living their dream, or living somebody else's dream. They are either creating value for themselves or for somebody else. They want the freedom to live their lives on their terms and reap the rewards and losses that flow from their decisions and efforts. They are willing to bet on themselves. But it is not for everyone. There are countless careers that I admire that offer some of the same rewards as owning or running a business, but to each their own. Our goal is not to suggest there is only one path; we just want to help guide you as you determine your path.

Your Health

Starting a business is a contact sport. If you do not take care of yourself, you won't be able to take care of your business. If you do not eat right, exercise, sleep, and take care of your overall conditioning, you will find yourself running out of energy and eventually desire. One of the biggest keys to success in any business is energy! You have to be able to create it and sustain it. When things go wrong, when you're tired and run down, you'll quickly find that the floodgates of fear and negative thoughts will start to kick in. Left unchecked, these feelings will start to overwhelm you and the abundance of negative thoughts can eventually lead to depression and despair. You should approach your business just like a professional athlete approaches his or her career: See your doctor, get a trainer, develop a plan, and go to work! Do whatever you have to do to make sure you can perform at your peak performance levels.

Your Finances

First, you need to clearly understand your monthly living expenses in detail. I don't just mean your mortgage and car payments, I mean everything. Do you spend $300 a month eating out? $150 a month on golf? What about car repairs? Health insurance? Holiday presents? Shopping? Write down everything you spend on a pad or in your smart phone over the course of 30 to 90 days. You will be amazed at how many small, trivial expenses will quickly add up to a few hundred dollars per month, and thousands of dollars over the course of a year. Do you have credit card debit? Do you have a home equity line to fall back on? Do you have 12 to 18 months living expenses set aside so you can focus on your business?

Before launching your business on a full-time basis, eliminate every expense you can, establish a cash reserve, and if possible establish a line of credit while you have steady income coming in. You can always add back in items as your business cash flow becomes more predictable. Just like with your health, you want to make sure your finances are as strong as possible. In many cases, this may require you to take on outside investors in order to achieve the level of financial stability you will need in order to successfully execute your business plans.

Your Alignment

We have developed what we call the "Life Vision Alignment Model" to enable you to gain a better understanding of how all these areas of your life drive how you are feeling. Once you establish your life's vision, decide on your career path, and true up your health and finances, the final step is to ensure alignment.

Alignment does not mean balance, as the *Life Vision Alignment Model* shows, it means:

Fulfillment

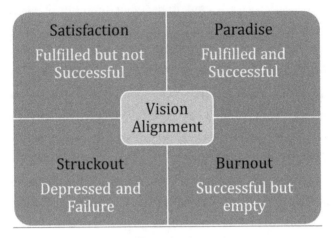

Emptiness

Through alignment, we move to a higher plane, one not based on success alone, but based on success and fulfillment. The reason most successful people burnout is because they are operating in the lower right hand quadrant, where they are successful based on external measures, but are internally empty and out of alignment with what they desire in their lives. The upper left quadrant is where you find many folks doing rewarding work, but work that just doesn't pay large amounts of money. They are fulfilled, but not successful by our traditional financial measures of success. The bottom left of the quadrant is where we find the people that are currently taking more from the system than they are actually contributing. The goal for most of us is to find success and fulfillment, or what we refer to as *paradise*.

Alignment gives us the opportunity to ensure our success comes with the fulfillment we desire, creating a sense of personal paradise. Only then will we live life in a centered and completely fulfilled manner.

What's the Right Fit for You?

You can't fail; you can only learn and grow. As Michael Jordan famously said, *"I've missed more than 9,000 shots in my career. I've lost almost 300 games. 26 times I've been trusted to take the game winning shot and missed. I've failed over and over and over again in my life. And that is why I succeed."*

What really matters the most to you? What does your ideal day, week, month, or year look like? What impact would you like to make in this world? How would you like to be remembered? These are the truly important questions that will help guide you towards locating paradise.

Successful people have many traits in common, but one commonality is their perception of failure. Thomas Watson, the founder of IBM, said, "If you want to be successful, just double your rate of failures."

Edison failed to invent the light bulb over 1,000 times. Successful people realize that failing is part of the process, and it is a required and necessary step along their path to achieving success. Each failure is welcomed as a chance to learn, a chance to grow, and a chance to move forward with more knowledge and experience.

People often ask us the same question: "What if I fail?" Our response, "What if you never try?" People seem so worried about what other people, who are not trying and not pursuing their dreams, will think of them. Personally, I (Dennis) still remember the comments I got almost two decades ago when I left a six-figure job to launch a company only a few short months after my son was born. People just seemed to assume a corporate job would somehow be a safer career path.

To fully live your life, you have to learn to embrace your fears and mistakes, learn from them, and continue forward! Always keep moving in the direction of your dreams. Always remember that many unexpected successes have been built on the foundation of failure and setbacks. You need to get in the game, and just get started by taking that first step.

How many times have you been sitting on your couch watching your favorite television show and during the commercial break you see it, right there on national TV, the very product idea you had just a few short months or years ago? You immediately think…that was my idea! They stole my idea!

I have no hard numbers to support this phenomenon, but my guess is that this scenario has played out millions of times a year across the globe. It's obvious that both you and a million other folks had the same problem, and in a passing moment thought of a similar solution. You all shared a common problem that eventually led some enterprising individual or company to capture and profit from that opportunity. It could have been you. Why wasn't it? That is the question that needs to be answered.

Years ago when seeking venture funding for one of my start-ups, a venture capitalist told me he saw business as either selling medicine or selling ice cream. Ice cream is nice to have, but you need medicine. The point he was making was simple: The bigger the problem, the greater the pain, the bigger the opportunity. If you want to get really rich, you just have to simply solve really big problems.

The Small Business Dilemma

The facts are daunting. Senator Rand Paul (R-KY) recently stated on CNN that "9 out of 10 businesses fail." Although, we can't find the data he used for that assertion, The Small Business Administration data shows that after 4 years, 50% of the businesses are still open and about 1/3 of those are still open after 10 years. The numbers are even scarier for what I call micro or solo entrepreneurs. These are the "work from home" folks entering MLM programs, selling digital products online, joining affiliate programs, or any other pay as you go business. In fact, a recent Facebook post by the JVZoo.com co-founder stated that 97% of product launches failed on their platform despite the fact that entrepreneurs on the JVZoo.com platform had achieved almost $100 million in sales.

The Internet age in which we live has made it very easy for anyone to buy a domain and launch a business for under $100. As a result, most people spent more time planning their yearly vacation than they did their business launch. Back in the 1990s it wasn't that easy. I had to raise $1 million dollars in funding just to build a data center to support our business launch. Back then, the only clouds in existence were the ones in the sky. Facing those kinds of hurdles, you had to have a well-thought-out plan or at least the ability to add .com to the end of your name. No one would give you any money, especially not enough to start a business, unless your plan was crystal clear.

Although most business studies cite lack of capital as a key reason businesses fail, the root causes run much deeper. Most business owners never clearly define their market's problems, understand why they are uniquely positioned to solve their market's problems, never fully master their niche, create the right solution for the market, or even enter into the right partnerships to support growth. Even when met with initial success, they fail to build a sustainable and scalable business. They never develop tools that allow them to monitor shifting consumer preferences, build repeatable processes, and establish a brand built on a real sustainable competitive advantage.

Building a Family Business

Many of the most famous and successful businesses in the U.S. are family-owned. Wal-Mart, Ford Motor, and Cargill are about as big as they come. Despite recessions, fluctuating consumer tastes, and bursting bubbles, these companies are able to maintain their family roots.

To last and remain relevant in the mind of the consumers, these businesses all continue to reinvent themselves over and over and over again. It is highly unlikely that your one big product idea is going to be enough to fuel the years of success you desire. You have to constantly adjust and align internally and externally.

Will the second, third, and fourth-generation family members be able to continually build on the foundation of the prior generation?

I grew up in a family business, where my dad and my grandfather were both plumbers. Way before I ever attended college, I was learning the delicate dynamics of combining family and business firsthand.

Here are some key concepts that can improve the success rates for future generations of any family business.

1. **Get family members involved early**. I remember riding in my dad's plumbing truck, tagging along on service calls, and hanging out at the shop from the time I was just seven or eight years old. It is amazing how much you can learn just by observing. I can remember times when I just wanted to hang out at the office with my dad instead of heading outside and playing with friends. I learned by watching.

2. **Learn the business from the bottom up.** Over the years, I have realized the importance of learning the business from as many positions as possible. When you understand all the components of your business, you understand how they synchronistically come together to deliver a unique customer experience. You understand how to perform each job, how to improve it, and how to control costs. After all, it is very difficult to manage a business if you don't understand key components that lead to your ultimate success.

3. **Share the same goals and values**. I was taught from a very young age to appreciate every customer. My dad would continually drive home the fact that we only have a business because of our customers. Providing our customers with an unwavering commitment to excellence aligned all of us. It was that mission and purpose that cut through the company's roots and supported our constant growth.

4. **Learn from past generations**. It is extremely important to create an environment where lessons learned from the past can be passed down to future generations. One method my dad used with me was to simply allow me to make decisions on my own. Afterwards, he would ask about my decision-making process and he would explain how he would have approached the decision, the factors he would have considered, and why those factors were important. The key was, he would only do this after I made the decisions, thereby allowing me to develop my own approaches and my own confidence in my decision-making abilities.

5. **Work harder than the others**. Many next generation owners feel entitled based on the past success of their family's business. They don't want to go out there and work hard and get their hands dirty. They coast and take the easy way out, which eventually leads to failure. In order to maintain a culture established by the founders, family members need to actually work harder than the other employees.

6. **Respect your shifting roles**. In one setting you're an employee, in another a son, and in another a brother. Wearing these different hats can be very difficult for family members to keep straight, but successful family businesses learn how to establish boundaries and never mix the business with the pleasure or displeasure.

7. **Grow the business**. The current generation running the company needs to stay open to new technologies and approaches. You must adopt a philosophy that you are either growing or you are dying. You have to balance tradition with evolution and growth, respecting the vision that built the business, but constantly tweaking to survive the changing tides.

8. **Balancing the family reputation**. Everyone needs to be aware of how his or her actions inside and outside of the business can reflect on the brand. It can be difficult to balance your individual identity, your family identity, and your business identity on a daily basis.

9. **Leave business at the office**. The key to maintaining balance between family and business is to treat each other with respect and leave the business at the office as much as is humanly possible. No matter what happens while on the job, do your best to instill a "leave it at the job" policy.

Keeping it in the Family

Although you may not know it, family businesses are economic powerhouses. They create jobs, pay taxes, and help build vibrant communities across the country.

- Family-owned businesses are the backbone of the American economy. Studies have shown about 35 percent of Fortune 500 companies are family-controlled and represent the full spectrum of American companies from small businesses to major corporations. In addition, family businesses account for 50 percent of U.S. gross domestic product, generate 60 percent of the country's employment, and account for 78 percent of all new job creation.[1]

- The greatest part of America's wealth lies with family-owned businesses. Family firms comprise 80 to 90 percent of all business enterprises in North America.[2]

- Roughly 90 percent of the families responding to a survey in "From Longevity of Firms to Trans-generational Entrepreneurship of Families: Introducing Family Entrepreneurial Orientation" indicated that they control more than a single firm. The results of the survey suggest that there is strong entrepreneurial activity undertaken by controlling families beyond their core (i.e., largest) company.[3]

- Small businesses, including many family firms, employ just over half of US workers. Of 119.9 million non-farm private sector workers in 2006, small firms with fewer than 500 workers employed 60.2 million, and large firms employed 59.7 million. Firms with fewer than 20 employees employed 21.6 million.[4]

- Research shows that family businesses are less likely to lay off employees regardless of financial performance.[5]

- More than 30% of all family owned businesses survive into the second generation. Twelve percent will still be viable into the third generation, with 3% of all family businesses operating at the fourth-generation level and beyond. [6]

- The tenure of leadership in a "Family Enterprise" is four to five times longer than their counterparts.[7]

  Of primary importance among family firm wealth holders is transferring not only their financial wealth, but also their values surrounding their wealth to subsequent generations. Primary values taught include encouraging children to earn their own money, philanthropy, charitable giving, and volunteering.[8]

- The environment for innovation in family businesses improves when more generations of the owning family are actively involved in the business.[9]

- The largest family-owned business in the US is Wal-Mart Inc., with $443.9 billion in net sales and 1.4 million U.S. employees in 2012.[10]

- In the S&P 500 companies, ROI is greater in family businesses, with a 6.65 percent higher return than non-family firms.[11]

- Women are increasingly participating in family businesses. Currently, 24 percent of family businesses are led by a female

CEO or President, and 31.3 percent of family businesses surveyed indicate that the next successor is a female. Nearly 60 percent of all family-owned businesses have women in top management team positions.[12]

- Of the non-family firms in the Fortune 1000, only 2.5 percent are currently led by women (Fortune Magazine, 2007).[13]

- By 2017, it is estimated that 40.3 percent of family business owners expect to retire, creating a significant transition of ownership in the US. Less than half of those expecting to retire in five years have selected a successor.[14]

- Even though nearly 70% of family businesses would like to pass their business on to the next generation, only 30% will actually be successful at transitioning to the next generation.[15]

Here are some of the most successful family businesses that can serve as examples as to just how big a family business can ultimately become:

Wal-Mart is the world's largest retailer and the most successful family business of all time, based on revenues. In 1962, founder Sam Walton opened the first Wal-Mart store in Rogers, Arkansas. After Walton died in 1992, his empire was passed on to his wife and children. Rob Walton succeeded his father as chairman of Wal-Mart, and his brother, John, served on a company committee that oversaw Wal-Mart's finances and future projects until his death in 2005. Walton's other children have distanced themselves from the family business, but remain important shareholders of the corporation.

Mars is one of the world's largest and most successful manufacturers of chocolate, confection, gum, drinks, and pet care products. Frank C. Mars started the candy giant in 1911, and it grew exponentially with the introduction of the incredibly popular Milky Way candy bar. His only son, Forrest Mars, who helped launch the brand internationally, later acquired the company. Although a non-family member runs Mars today, the company still remains in the Mars family name and its members make up the board of directors.

Comcast is the largest cable operator and home Internet service provider in the United States. It's also one of the biggest and most successful family-owned companies of all time. Founder Ralph J. Roberts transformed Comcast Corporation from a small, Mississippi cable-TV business to a billion-dollar media empire.

Ford Motor Company is the second-largest automaker in the U.S. and one of the biggest family businesses of all time. Ford's rich history begins with its legendary founder, Henry Ford, whose innovation and strong leadership led to the creation of the first affordable automobile, the Ford Model T. For more than 100 years, the Ford family has maintained control of the automotive company. The founder's great-grandson, William Clay Ford, Jr., currently serves as the executive chairman and two other family members sit on the board.

Cargill is a private agriculture business that specializes in the manufacture and distribution of crops and livestock. William W. Cargill founded the company in 1865 and, with the help of his two brothers, Cargill Inc. transformed from a small grain storage facility in the Midwest to a major producer and marketer of agricultural and industrial goods and services. Although Cargill hired its first non-family member as CEO, the descendants of William W. Cargill still own more than 85% of the company.

Bechtel Corporation is the largest engineering company in the United States, best known for helping in the construction of the Hoover Dam, as well as the BART system, and the Channel Tunnel. Since its creation in 1898, Bechtel has always functioned as a family-owned business. This family empire has faced a great deal of criticism for its project choices, privacy restrictions, and political clout.

Brothers Paul and Joseph Galvin founded Motorola in 1928, and together they launched the first commercial car radio, called the

Motorola. In 1959, Paul's son, Robert Galvin, took over the company and oversaw the production of DynaTac, the first cellular phone. His son, Chris, ran Motorola from 1997 to 2003, before being excommunicated by the board and replaced by a non-family member. Although the Galvin family has lost control of the company in recent years, it will always go down in history as one of the biggest and most successful family businesses.

Putting it Together

So what does this mean for you? The hope for this chapter was to give you some of the crucial elements to consider when beginning a business. It is great to think about quitting your day job and opening up your dream business, but unless you are retirement ready, there will likely be substantial risk. Your job is to properly plan and implement strategies to reduce that risk, while understanding exactly what you are getting yourself into.

For us, starting a small family business was the product of a diagnosis. The journey began as a hobby, and quickly turned into a greater opportunity. It has grown with the help of our son, and he has played an integral role in its mission and vision. But we still try to instill proper business practices into his mind and into our business, even though he isn't the one taking the risk.

As we continue along the journey through this book, we will begin to focus on the specific type of business that we opened. But the fundamental lessons and considerations we discussed before opening our business were outlined within this chapter. One of the most powerful steps we took was to create a rock-solid "Life Vision Alignment Model," which eventually guided us in the direction of our dreams.

We didn't open our business out of necessity; we did it out of love. And the same may be true for you. Whatever your driving force may be, once your doors open, you better be prepared for what's to come. It can be a bumpy road ahead, even if you have planned for years. So with that said, we fully support the idea of opening your own business, but only if you are well-prepared and ready to be a business owner. Now it is time to open the garage-doors of opportunity and discuss how we became *Resale Millionaires.*

Chapter 3

HAPPINESS IS THE WAY:
Building Success

For us, it was tragedy, not happiness that catapulted us into the world of garage sales and owning a small business. It was not something for which we planned or intended to enter into. It was literally a byproduct of cancer. But sometimes it is tragedy that ultimately shines the light on, and opens the door for, happiness. Cancer pushed us to take a step back, realize we are all on a limited clock, and then analyze and evaluate if the lives we were collectively living truly made us happy. After examining our lives under a very lucid microscope, we understood that we were creating our own circumstances and there was so much more in store for us. It was through that scrutiny and analysis that we began to really shift to a concerted and calculated desire to not only live a happy life, but also to understand how happiness really works.

This chapter will begin by discussing the idea of happiness, and then transition into how to apply your newly found happiness into the structure for a small business. We will discuss some of the most important questions you can ask in the initial phase, and then identify exactly what you should address before you open your doors.

Happiness on the Mind

The human brain receives eleven million pieces of information every second from the environment, yet it can only process forty bits per second, which means it has to quickly determine which tiny percentage of inputs to process. Your brain is literally dismissing the majority of the inputs it receives.[16] In truth, there really is more than one reality. There are actually millions of realities your brain could construct every second. Your reality all depends on what gets past your brain's filters. The more interpretations of the world that can pass your brain's filters, the better you can construct your life's vision alignment to achieve real fulfillment and happiness.

But what does this have to do with starting your own business and our love for garage sales?

As we write this section, we can look out our office window and see a number of different things: the yard, the trees, and even the lake. As our brain processes all kinds of things, which the eye can see, we may eventually focus on one object, for example a tree. We can then see the circumference of the tree, the bark of the tree, part of the shadow of the tree, and much more. What we can't see is the actual height of the tree, all the branches, the sides and rear of the tree, and even the root system. We can make many assumptions about the tree, but it is not until we gain different vantage points that we can truly understand all that are part of this harmonious piece of Mother Nature. But it doesn't end there: If we were to climb the tree we would gain even more insights about it, and if we were to start to dig around the base of the tree we would gain further insights, and if we were to cut down the tree we could count the rings and learn the tree's approximate age.

By looking for more vantage points of the tree, we begin to create more realities. The same is true within our own lives. The more realities we can see, the better we will become at making decisions that will move us toward those realities that offer us lasting happiness. If you don't have a good understanding of your current reality, there is little chance you will achieve true happiness. You simply need to move from your current position and look for a different vantage point. Once we can see and construct a reality that is aligned with our life's vision, we can start to train our brain to filter out more of the noise and eventually manifest a reality that will lead to greater happiness and success in our lives.

What Can a Dress Teach Us About Happiness?

It turns out, quite a lot. It all began on February 26, 2015, when Grace MacPhee of Scotland posted a photo of a dress, asking her followers to comment on what colors they saw. She initially got into a disagreement over the dress's color with her mother, who thought the dress was white and gold. However, MacPhee was intent that the dress was black and blue. Once the photo was posted on Tumblr, a social media site, the debate quickly spread to Twitter, where people aggressively split into two opposing camps: #teamblueandblack and #teamwhiteandgold. By the next day, it seemed the whole world had an opinion on #TheDress.

Even Philadelphia police weighed in, tweeting: "WANTED: This dress to stop appearing in our feed (Even though we'd look simply ravishing in it) #BlueAndBlack." *How could a simple debate over a dress create so much discord across the globe?* Some talked about the different factors that played into the significant split like age, gender, and your mental state of being. If you saw blue and black, it was because you were stressed, but if you saw white and gold, it was because you were viewing the picture from an android device.

Alongside "The Dress," MacPhee also got her 15 minutes of fame and ended up on "The Ellen DeGeneres Show." We now know that "The

Dress" is in fact blue and black, but does that even matter? The debate was never intended to be about a trick of the eye or mind, or to even fuel a worldwide debate—it was simply an honest question as to color.

If we were to look at happiness as a dress color, I may never know if my experience of blue and black is different from your experience of blue and black, but surely I can tell that my experience of blue and black is different from my experience of white and gold when I compare the two, right?

Unfortunately, this too is subject to debate. It turns out we are at best comparing something we are currently experiencing with the memory of something we experienced in the past. In one study, researchers showed volunteers a color swatch and allowed them to study it for five seconds.[17] Some volunteers then spent thirty seconds describing the color (describers), while other volunteers did not describe it (non-describers). All volunteers were then shown a lineup of six color swatches, one of which was the color they had seen thirty seconds earlier, and were then asked to pick out the original swatch.

Only 73% of the non-describers were able to identify it accurately, in other words, fewer than three quarters could tell if their experience of yellow was the same experience they had of yellow only thirty seconds earlier. Even more surprising was the fact that only 33 percent of those who had described the color accurately identified the original color. Apparently, their verbal descriptions of the color had "overwritten" their memories of their experiences, and it is our experiences that play a critical role in how we perceive and interpret the world around us.

As a young girl growing up in Central California, great weather was something I just took for granted, especially now that we have lived in Chicago, Illinois for a period of time. On one particular morning in my early 20s, I was going to college part-time and working three jobs to make ends meet. During the week I worked as a chiropractic assistant;

on weekends I worked as a wine hostess at a local winery; and at night, I cleaned office buildings with the little energy I had left. As a twenty-year-old, I wanted to go to my happy place every chance I could: the peace and serenity of the beach.

So you can only imagine how I felt when it rained on my one day off for weeks. I was really beside myself. Needing to clear my head, I decided I would go for a drive. As I listened to the radio, the DJ was very excited about the rain and he went on and on about how the farmers in the area were in desperate need of the rain and how excited these farmers were since many relied significantly on rain to water their crops. The very rain that had ruined my day had been a godsend for so many others.

At that moment, a light bulb went off in my head. I realized it was just weather! The rain was neither good or bad—it was just weather. At that point in my life, I did not understand the power of vantage points, but I did understand it was how we reacted to the rain and our unique perspective that assigned meaning to it. Our personal filters led us to perceive the rain as either good or bad. I wanted to go to the beach that day, so for me, the rain was unwelcomed and disappointing. But from the farmer's vantage point, they were overjoyed and filled with happiness by that very same rain.

Our experiences and vantage points instantly become a part of the lens through which we view our past, present, and future, and even shape and distort what we see. Understanding this simple principle is the key to achieving lasting happiness. *Webster's* defines happiness as "a feeling or state of well-being and contentment." While technically accurate, we find the words of Dinesh D'Souza much more useful, *"Happiness is a journey, not a destination. For a long time it seemed to me that life was about to begin—real life. But there was always some obstacle in the way, something to be gotten through first, some unfinished business, time still to be served, and a debt to be paid.*

At last it dawned on me that these obstacles were my life. This perspective has helped me to see there is no way to happiness. Happiness is the way. So treasure every moment you have and remember that time waits for no one."

We have also discovered that happiness is not a fixed point, a destination with a known GPS coordinate, or an address you can just enter into your device of choice and select the "quickest route." Happiness is in fact a journey, one that constantly ebbs and flows. Once we understood this reality, a major breakthrough and transformation occurred in our lives. Happiness is what fueled our desire to leave the rat race and to start a family business, even in the face of all the completely reasonable fears we experienced.

Below are some stories of families who also have unique and inspirational stories at the intersection of happiness and business.

The Unexpected Path to Happiness

Prior to the 1970 National Football League draft, on the campus of Louisiana State University, two young men's paths significantly diverged. You probably are familiar with NFL great Terry Bradshaw, who went on to become the number one pick in the 1970 NFL Draft. Bradshaw had a fourteen-year career with the Pittsburgh Steelers. His career highlights include four Super Bowl victories, two Super Bowl MVPs, Sports Illustrated Sportsman of the Year, and election into the Football Hall of Fame.

But you likely have heard little of Phil Robertson, who was ahead of Bradshaw on Louisiana Tech's depth chart, but gave up football with one year of eligibility remaining because football interfered with his true passion: duck-hunting.

Bradshaw wrote in his autobiography, *It's Only a Game*: "The quarterback playing ahead of me, Phil Robertson, loved hunting more than he loved football. He'd come to practice directly from the woods, squirrel tails hanging out of his pockets, duck feathers on his clothes. Clearly he was a fine shot, so no one complained too much."

When asked about Bradshaw's comments, Robertson has said, "You gotta remember, my heart was then and to this day—let me put it this way: Throwing a touchdown pass to a guy running down the sideline, and he runs down with the ball for six, it was fun. However, in my case, it was much more fun to be standing down in some flooded timber with about 35 or 40 mallard ducks comin' down on top of me in the woods. That did my heart more good than all the football in the world."

Robertson went to work as a schoolteacher for several years after graduating from Tech, obtaining his master's degree in education via night classes and enjoying each and every duck-hunting season!

With all his time in the woods, Robertson became more and more dissatisfied with the available commercial duck calls, so like any good entrepreneur, he set out to start producing and selling his own duck calls. He began his business in a dilapidated shed, where he spent 25 years making duck calls from Louisiana cedar trees.

In his first year, Robertson said he sold $8,000 worth of duck calls. Today, Robertson's company, Duck Commander, has sales in the millions, with contracts in outdoor stores across the United States and a hit TV show "Duck Dynasty" on the A&E Network. For the past decade, the Robertson's third son Willie has been their CEO, which his parents say was an obvious choice.

"He was about 10 or 11, junior high; they called us from school, he had set up a concession stand, selling candies, and he absolutely shut down the school's whole snack shop," Kay Robertson said. "I said, 'he's our CEO,'" Phil added.[18]

The company is still very much all in the family, with roughly 80 percent of its employees being related, one way or another, to the Robertson clan.

Keeping it in the Family

The Zoppè family has been focused on delivering happiness for over 170 years, across six generations, by bringing an old-time family circus to the world. The Zoppè Family Circus emerged from humble beginnings more than 170 years ago to become one of the most legendary circuses in all of Europe. And like many good legends, it all began with a boy and a girl falling in love.

In 1842, a young French street performer named Napoline Zoppè wandered into a plaza in Budapest, Hungary, looking for work. There, his eyes glanced upon a beautiful equestrian ballerina named Ermenegilda, who captured the hearts and minds of the crowd with her grace and showmanship. More importantly, this talented beauty captured Napoline's heart.

However, since Napoline was a clown, Ermenegilda's father saw him as beneath her and disapproved of their relationship. The two ran away to Venice, Italy, and founded the circus that still bears their name. Over the generations, the circus survived wars and political upheaval in Italy and throughout the rest of Europe.

Alberto Zoppè believes it's the audience that keeps circus performers like him young and in the ring. "When you see that somebody loves what you're doing, you enjoy it even more," Alberto says. "I was born into show business, so I don't think I'm going to get out of it before I die. I'm 82 now, and I've got an artificial hip and an artificial knee, but I still don't want to get out."[19]

Pursuing your passions is not just a family affair either; some of the greatest businesses have been built when someone decided to pursue their own personal vision. Consider the outcomes from these examples of pioneers and trailblazers that followed their happiness, their passion, and their hearts:

- *In June 2005, Steve Jobs took the podium at Stanford Stadium to give the commencement speech to Stanford's graduating class. Wearing jeans and sandals under his formal robe, Jobs addressed a crowd of 23,000 with a short speech that drew lessons from his life. About a third of the way into the address, Jobs offered the following advice: "You've got to find what you love...the only way to do great work is to love what you do. If you haven't found it yet, keep looking, and don't settle."*

- *Richard Branson is the only entrepreneur to have built eight separate billion-dollar companies in eight different industries— and he did it all without a degree in business. Branson has said "Entrepreneurship is about turning what excites you into capital, so that you can do more of it and with it."*

- *Nobel Prize winner Albert Schweitzer continuously reached for truth, peace, freedom and humanity. He fought for prosecuted and threatened people again and again. When asked about happiness he said: "Success is not the key to happiness. Happiness is the key to success. If you love what you are doing, you will be successful."*

- *Entrepreneur Mary Kathlyn Wagner (Mary Kay) was born on May 12, 1918, in Hot Wells, Texas. Mary was a pioneer for women in business, building a substantial cosmetics empire. In 1939, Mary Kay became a salesperson for Stanley Home Products, hosting parties to encourage people to buy household items. She was so good at making the sale that she was hired away by another company, World Gifts, in 1952. Mary Kay spent a little more than a decade at the company, but she quit in protest after watching yet another man that she had trained get promoted above her and earn a much higher salary than hers. After her bad experiences in the traditional workplace, Mary Kay set out to create her own business at the age of 45. She started with an initial investment of $5,000 in 1963. She purchased the formulas for skin lotions from the family of a* *tanner who created the products while he worked on hides. With her son, Richard Rogers, she opened a small store in Dallas and had nine salespeople working for her. Today Mary Kay's sales top $3.5 billion, employ some 5,000 workers, and their products are sold in more than 35 markets around the world with a global independent sales force in excess of 3 million people. When asked to reflect on life she said, "Most people live and die with their music still unplayed. They never dare to try."*

Robertson, Jobs, Branson, Schweitzer, Mary Kay, and countless other individuals who have found happiness have done so by actively seeking to create the life they envision. They turned their backs on the status quo and found the courage to believe they should follow their dreams. Our hope for you is that our story will help begin a shift in your life. It shouldn't take a life-altering event like cancer to make you pause and decide whether great change is needed in your life. The reality is that if you are happy, everything will fall into place, and if you are unhappy, your life will remain completely unfulfilled.

For years we were both bothered by our lack of understanding of what would truly bring lasting happiness into our lives. The new job made us happy for six months to a year, before the daily grind and stress started to outweigh the happiness and joy we felt just a short time earlier. We experienced the same thing with the new cars, new houses, new sets of golf clubs, new outfits, new cities, new jewelry, and countless other purchases throughout the years. It seemed that true happiness was fleeting, something we could experience in bursts, moments in time, but never everlasting. We wondered what was wrong with us? How could something that made us happy just a few months or years earlier now be the very source of our unhappiness? When we tried to talk to others about our experiences we got replies like "Join the club;" "It's called life;" and even, "You just need to grow up."

Why had everyone given up on happiness?

Why had they stopped dreaming, stopped believing, and stopped living?

As kids we were always advised to avoid discussing the big three: Religion, Politics, and Money. As adults, happiness and fulfillment shot to the top of that list. It was like we had entered a "no fly zone," strictly guarded and protected with orders to shoot down anyone or anything that approached. It occurred to us that happiness and fulfillment were the equivalent of the government's "Area 51:" We all have heard about it, we know it exists, we have had glimpses of it, but it remains a deeply guarded secret. It is no wonder America ranks only #17 in the United Nations' Survey of the World's Happiest Countries.[20] Our attitudes and aptitudes towards happiness have to change.

Creating a Happy Life—Live Like You Are Dying

Mark Twain famously said, *"Twenty years from now you will be more disappointed by the things that you didn't do than by the ones you did do. So throw off the bowlines. Sail away from the safe harbor. Catch the trade winds in your sails. Explore. Dream. Discover."* For us, that is happiness: taking chances, accepting opportunity, and following our heart and souls in the direction of that which feels right.

Bronnie Ware is an Australian nurse who spent several years working in palliative care, caring for patients in the last 12 weeks of their lives. Ware writes of the phenomenal clarity of vision that people gain at the end of their lives, and how we might learn from their wisdom. "When questioned about any regrets they had or anything they would do differently," she says, "common themes surfaced again and again."

Here are the top five regrets of the dying:

1. I wish I'd had lived my dreams, not the life society expected of me.
2. I wish I hadn't worked so hard.

3. I wish I'd had the courage to express my feelings.
4. I wish I had stayed in touch with my friends.
5. I wish that I had let myself be happier.

What would you do right now if you learned that you were going to die in the next week, month or year? Would you rush to the office to make sure you could get that current project done? Would you seek to spend more time with your family and friends? Would you toss that diet you are on out the window? Would you look to mend a broken relationship? Would you totally throw caution to the wind and do something completely out of character? For each of us the answers will be different, but we are willing to bet your actions would change drastically based on whether your time horizon was a week, month or year. The things we do are naturally based on our perception of the time we have left. We spend most of the hours of most of our days planning the *tomorrows* we hope will make us happy after tomorrow. You see the issue? We are willing to endure a lot of pain today for the hope of a better future that we may never see.

Anthony Burgess was just 40 when he was told that he had less than a year to live because of a brain tumor. With nothing in savings, he worried about his wife and what her life would look like.

He struggled with what he might do to provide for her future in such a short period of time. For years, he had wanted to be a writer. In fact, there was this voice in his head that said he could be a great writer. Unfortunately, Anthony had never listened to that voice before. But now that he was dying, he hoped he could write a book that might create a stream of royalties for his wife after he was gone.

With no other practical options surfacing, Anthony spent the next 9 months writing day and night, finishing an amazing five and a half novels. That's more than most writers create in a decade. Talk about cramming a life's work into just a few months.

Although this is an incredible feat, it isn't the most exciting part of Anthony's story. While he was busy chasing his dreams, his cancer miraculously disappeared.

Anthony's story doesn't end there, as he would go on to a long and distinguished life as a novelist. Anthony Burgess wrote more than 70 books, including the famous *A Clockwork Orange*. In 2005, *A Clockwork Orange* was included on *Time* magazine's list of the 100 best English-language novels written since 1923.[21] Unbelievably, without his death sentence, he may never have written at all.

What's your greatest regret so far? What will you set out to achieve or change before you die?

The answers may not at first seem obvious, so you need to devote time to thinking seriously about how to spend your life and how much of it you can actually enjoy. That is truly what happiness is all about: taking the time to figure out what makes you tick, and then creating a life around it.

You may have noticed one glaring omission in the previous chapter—we never told you our life's vision statement. That omission was not lost on us, as we felt it was better placed here as a way to more fully tie things together for you:

> *"To continually take on new challenges*
> *and pursue our sense of purpose in life."*

That is what happiness means to us. Notice the subtle use of the word "sense." This simple word makes all the difference in our happiness. It is our sense of purpose, not our actual single purpose. When you understand that happiness is a journey and an evolving continuum, you can then understand your purpose is a journey as well. When you remove the absolute, or the fixed point in time and space as a true and forever constant, you can begin to understand that you are being shaped by your experiences and your interpretation of those experiences. As such, it is your sense of those experiences that will guide you and allow you to truly be happy.

Through this paradigm, you start to understand the house, the car, and the job are really no different than the toys that made you happy in your childhood. You know, the ones that you disregarded after playing with for just a few minutes. But think about that one stuffed-animal or blanket you took with you everywhere. It was comforting, warming, loving, and it made you feel safe. You just couldn't live without it. That, for us, is happiness.

As we become adults, we take on responsibilities, and we lose our ability to build and even maintain a happy life. We have been programmed by society to focus on creating stability, security, and making a living—not on making a life. And that is precisely where we lose our ability to be happy.

Happiness Manifests Itself in Business and Life

Earlier on, we promised we would tie the idea of happiness to beginning a small business. There's no doubt that passion is an important key to success, but in order to build a profitable business, you need to offer something for which others are looking. After all, the marketplace is not focused on the fact that you're following your passion. Consumers spend money on products or services that fill a particular need or desire. If there is no customer need or desire, your business won't last long, regardless of your passion and grand vision.

If you decided that starting a business is for you, you will face many questions to which you absolutely need the answers. Your ability to successfully answer these questions will be a significant key in achieving your ultimate success. Regardless of whether you are looking to start a business, launch a new career, or just improve your current situation, a great place to start is to ask yourself this question:

What do you believe you could excel at and enjoy for a long period of time?

Remember, any small business should live at the intersection of that which makes you happy and that which you are successful at.

Once you have answered the question above, you'll likely have a compass in which to guide your path forward. Additionally, learning to ask good questions is one of the most important skills you can develop not just while building your business, but also while building your life. Learning to ask the right questions is one of the most overlooked factors in achieving happiness and success.

Remember Phil Robertson of Duck Commander fame? Well, he tells one story in his book *Happy, Happy, Happy* that drives home the critical nature of asking questions. Robertson had procured a loan for $25,000 to purchase machinery to launch his business. He ran across an ad for a lathe in the back of a magazine so he called the seller to learn more. The seller asked him how much money he had to spend, and Robertson replied, "Well, I only have twenty-five thousand." The man replied that the equipment was only $24,985. He found out later the equipment he purchased was worth only five thousand dollars— Robertson had been fleeced. This one event was the reason he was so poor in the early years of his business.[22] That one question gave the crook all the information he needed to take complete and full advantage of Robertson.

With that in mind, let's look at some of the key questions, and ultimately the decisions, you will have to make once you decide to launch your business. From our perspective, we believe there are nine distinct and crucial questions you have to answer before you begin your business. By evaluating each of these questions in great detail, you will find yourself well-positioned to first determine if opening your own business is the right decision for you and, if so, planting the seeds and building the foundation for success early on.

These questions include:

1. *How Will You Organize Your Business?*
2. *How Will You Fund Your Business?*
3. *How Do You Identify a Good Business Opportunity?*
4. *What Differentiates Your Businesses Products or Services?*
5. *How Do You Design and Build Your Product or Service?*
6. *Who is Your Ideal Customer?*
7. *How Will Your Customers Find You?*
8. *How Will You Make Money?*
9. *How Will You Scale Your Business?*

Now that we have our list, let's dive headfirst into each of these nine questions.

Question # 1: How Will You Organize Your Business?

Organizing your business and staying compliant with local, state, and federal laws is not just a good idea, it is a legal requirement. Before you even order your first widget or provide your first consult, it is imperative you seek professional guidance in choosing which legal entity you will need. Forming a corporation is an absolute necessity, as it can protect you from significant financial and legal exposure. An attorney can work with you to ensure your legal entity is consistent with your business objectives.

For instance, if you plan to raise external capital, your attorney will likely recommend a C corporation. They may also recommend you form your legal entity in Delaware, as this structure may provide you with a more beneficial corporate law structure than other states. Your attorney may recommend you place any intellectual property or patent in a separate company from your operating company to reduce financial risk due to any infringement claims that may arise during the course of your business. The sky is the limit and if your attorney can imagine it, he likely can help you create it.

For most small businesses, your attorney will likely recommend an LLC or an S corporation to start, as these entities typically provide you with pass-through tax benefits, as well as maximum protection of your personal assets if you are sued. In recent years, LLCs have become popular because the record keeping requirements to keep your entity in good standing are typically much easier than their counterparts. The critical point is that you work with professional advisors to make sure you are setting up the right structure to meet your current and future needs.

You will also need a business checking account to ensure you maintain separation over your personal and businesses expenses. Utilizing separate accounts is often required by law to keep your corporation in good standing. These small yet pivotal steps are the gold standard for starting a new business and absolutely have to be tended to before you get things moving.

As a business, you will also likely have monthly, quarterly, and yearly state and federal reporting requirements. In addition, you will have various taxes to collect, submit, and pay. You will also want to work with a professional insurance broker to ensure you are fully covered for things like liability, errors and omissions, inventory, equipment, and vehicles. These are just a few of the initial considerations you should undertake before you open the doors to your new business. There are many more. And it is through books like this, and the professionals with which you surround yourself, that you can easily navigate these otherwise choppy waters. Our point is that you don't know what you don't know, so take the time to work with people that can shed the proverbial light on your new business.

Question # 2: How Will You Fund Your Business?

I often hear successful entrepreneurs say it will take twice as long and cost twice as much to make your business a success than what you initially planned. At first this may seem like the result of poor planning, but you have to realize that at the point you start your business, you have the least amount of information about your business. You are working under many assumptions about your product and services, and your customers have yet to offer little real results or feedback. You may find a market opportunity you never knew existed, you may find competitors respond to your offering in an unanticipated manner, or you may find some of your assumptions were just plain wrong. It is that learning curve that can cost you more than you ever imagined.

When we co-founded a plumbing company, we never intended to do gas work, but one of our customers needed help so we took a look at the opportunity. That opportunity later turned out to be one of our largest single accounts, and provided us with a unique position in the marketplace—one that drew the attention of a public company that eventually purchased the business for seven figures.

When launching a business, cash flow is the lifeblood of your organization. The number of days of cash on hand is a critical number for you to know. Most healthy small businesses typically have six to twelve months of cash to ensure they can survive an economic downturn or a large unexpected expense. If your business is seasonal, you face even more uncertainty from factors like inventory availability, consumer confidence, and even weather.

So when it comes to cash, we do believe it is a great idea to take your cash need and double it. This simple rule will allow you to extend your runway for success. I like to think of my business like an airplane taking off. A Cessna 172 needs only about 500 to 800 feet to take off, but the aircraft's weight is a key variable in the distance it will require for liftoff.

A heavily loaded 172 can require as much as three times the runway as a near empty plane. Additionally, outside air temperature makes a big impact on the ability to take off. On a hot day, you may need 200 to 500 feet more runway, and may not be able to take off at all if you are too heavy.

Field elevation plays a big role as well, as some airports may be more than 5000 feet above sea level, resulting in less lift from your wings, and subsequently requiring more runway. Weather can help or hurt you. A good stiff headwind might save you 200 or 300 feet from your takeoff roll, but you may face a crosswind, which will make it more difficult. What surface are you taking off from? Pavement reduces friction; taking off from grass usually requires 100 feet or more of runway. In short, there are lots of factors to consider. The same is true in business. On any given day, these factors are absolutely unpredictable. So always assume you need the longest runway, or the greatest amount of cash you could ever need. Otherwise, you are simply setting yourself up for a crash landing, if you even take off at all.

Question # 3: How Do You Identify a Good Business Opportunity?

There is no single way to evaluate a business opportunity. We like to understand the costs involved to prove the model, with the rule of thumb being the lower the better. We like to understand if the opportunity solves a big problem, or if it is just nice to have. We like to understand how well the business aligns with our vision, strengths, and weaknesses. We like to understand the competition: is it Wal-Mart or Uncle Buck's Homegoods? Does the business have a reoccurring revenue stream where clients pay a fixed fee every month, or do we start at zero each and every day, looking for new business? What type of labor do we require to run the business: skilled, semi-skilled, or not skilled at all? We can tell you one of the more difficult places to find yourself is in a business that requires a semi-skilled workforce. Many of the good workers have moved up the line to be skilled workers, and you will often find your ability to attract, train, and maintain this type of workforce very taxing.

Ask yourself, is this opportunity a product or a business? Many people think they are launching a business when in fact they are launching a product. If we were asked to boil all this down to one simple formula, a formula you could use as a short cut to save you time and money, it would be this:

$$\textbf{\textit{Problem + Pain = Opportunity}}$$

Opportunity is often disguised as a problem causing people pain. As a general rule, the bigger the problem means more people are experiencing the pain, which leads to bigger opportunity in the business realm. When it comes to evaluating opportunities, we usually follow a life lesson we taught our son Bradley: In the long run, the easy way is the hard way and the hard way is the easy way! There is little substitute for common sense and hard work; short cuts usually lead you to a very expensive dead end.

Question # 4: What Differentiates Your Businesses Products or Services?

Another way of asking this question is: What will be your unique position in the market? How will your plumbing company, restaurant, or Jet Ski rental business be different than the current choices in the market? Will you have a better price, location, or product offering? Will you be faster? Will you deliver better quality for the same price? If you are planning on selling a commodity-based product and you cannot compete on price, you are likely to fail in the long run. If you are reselling a well known consumer brand that Amazon sells direct to consumers, you are likely to fail unless you can do it quicker and for less. Fat chance, right? If you are launching a new industry and you have to educate your consumers on your product, you are likely to fail without having very deep pockets. If you are launching a product or service that operates in a highly fragmented industry, or solves a big problem or consumer pain, you likely have a winner on your hands.

Fragmentation usually means you have many opportunities to really differentiate and diversify your business. Reselling national brands limits your ability to differentiate yourself unless customer support, design, or other value added services are an integral part of the product life cycle. Carving out a niche service for national chains is one of the most effective ways to quickly scale and grow your business. Of course, doing so at a profit can be a major challenge.

Question # 5: How Do You Design and Build Your Product or Service?

You should not get caught up in offering everything to everybody. The reality is, you will not be able to launch your business with every bell and whistle you would like to have. The old saying goes that when you stand in the middle of the road, you get hit by traffic going both ways. Make sure you decide what you are, who you are, and what you will sell or offer. The goal should be to onboard paying customers as fast as possible and start receiving feedback to improve your product offerings. There are three things you must accomplish in order to launch with what has been coined a "Minimum Viable Product," and they are as follows:

1. The customer must be willing to pay for your product or service.
2. The product or service needs to create some value for the customer.
3. The product or service needs to be significant enough for you to gain critical feedback to test your key business assumptions.

As Einstein once said, "Everything should be made as simple as possible, but not simpler." Our experience has taught us that the quicker you can get things in customers' hands with fewer moving parts and variables, the greater your chances of success. All the planning, research and pre-launch work should be designed to not only get the product in your customer's hands quickly, but also to allow you to verify all the critical assumptions you have made about the drivers of your business.

Question # 6: Who is Your Ideal Customer?

I remember when I reviewed a business plan for some inspiring entrepreneurs. They had done an amazing job identifying their target customer demographic data, and had even created very specific personas for each type of customer. The work was very impressive, but there was one problem: their customers had no money. They had identified a problem and a pain, had come up with a great way to solve the problem, but did not realize there was no way to monetize their solution because no one could pay for it. They had not asked the question, "Can my target customer afford my solution?" Your ideal customer must be somebody who has a need, but they also need to be able to afford to pay for your solution.

Other key questions to ask and answer when identifying your ideal customers are:

- ✓ Does your customer have a compelling reason to buy?
- ✓ What will make your customer switch to your product or service?
- ✓ What will make them pick up the phone and call you, or click buy on your website?
- ✓ Are you offering a complete solution or just a part of a bigger solution?

For instance, if you are a subcontractor, your customer may actually be the general contractor hired by the end consumer, not the end consumer themselves. Make sure to clearly identify your customer base to ensure you will make a profit.

Question # 7: How Will Your Customers Find You?

In the movie "Field of Dreams," Ray Kinsella, played by Kevin Costner, is an Iowa farmer who lives with his wife Annie and his daughter Karin. While walking through his cornfield one night, Ray hears a voice that whispers, "If you build it, he will come." Ray continues hearing the voice before finally seeing a vision of a baseball diamond in his field. His wife Annie is a bit concerned by his vision, but ultimately concedes and allows her husband to plow down his corn fields in favor of a baseball field in the middle of nowhere Iowa. Ray's decision puts his family in a desperate position. Despite all his efforts, no one has come to his field. His community, friends, and family think he has gone nuts, and the bank is ready to foreclose on the farm—his family faces financial ruin.

However, one night, Karin eventually spots a uniformed man in the field who turns out to be Shoeless Joe Jackson. Jackson later returns from the cornfield with other deceased players banned in the 1919 Black Sox scandal. The movie has a typical Hollywood happy ending, and the "if you build it, he will come" narrative was certainly a winning formula for the movie. But in the realm of business, this couldn't be further from the right choice. In fact, it is likely a recipe for failure.

If you are going to be successful, you have to have a cost effective way for your customers to find out about you. Your plan should be very tactical and break down specific marketing channels like: affiliates, retargeting, radio, television, newspapers, email, direct mail, social media, content marketing, coupons, webinars, seminars, partnerships, feet on the street, and other approaches to get your message in front of your ideal customers.

In our best-selling book, *Ultimate Marketing Hacks: 241 Proven Marketing Hacks That Ignite Sales and Allow You to Dominate Your Competition,* we cover a wide array of low cost and no cost methods to attract customers and grow your business. After all, without paying customers, you really can't have a business very long.

Question # 8: How Will You Make Money?

When we ask aspiring entrepreneurs or business owners how they plan to make money, the answer is usually something along these lines: We are going to buy our product for $50 and mark it up X percent. This is often referred to as the "Cost Plus model." This approach is certainly not uncommon, but we want you to really think about the possibilities when designing your business model. They are endless, and you can even form a hybrid of two different models. The point is to open your eyes to the opportunities and give yourself the information and knowledge needed to make the right decision for you and your new business. Here are some ideas to get you thinking:

1. **Usage Fees**—Think utility companies that meter water and electric usage. Also, many cloud computing companies charge based on bandwidth and storage space utilized.

2. **Subscription Based**—This is one of our favorite models. Think monthly gym memberships, lawn care, pest control, etc. Customers sign up and continue to pay until their contract term expires. Pay a lot of attention to this model and try to figure out any opportunity to build a recurring revenue stream for your business. Service companies have gotten very good at selling preventative maintenance agreements to smooth out their monthly income stream.

3. **Shared Savings**—This is often used by companies who can lower your operating costs. Think cell phone bills, office

equipment rentals, etc. They lower your expenses and then receive a percentage of what they save you.

4. **Transaction Fees**—This is a model used by many online marketplaces like eBay and Amazon; you sell your item, and pay them a percentage of the transaction total.

5. **Advertising**—Build a popular blog or website, and you can charge advertisers to gain access to your audience via banner ads, emails, or maybe even your newsletter.

6. **Pay to Play**—This approach is widely used in the gaming community where users download a game for free, but in order to advance levels or speed up progress you need to buy particular tokens, tools, or powers.

7. **Consumables**—Often your product or service uses consumables like printer ink or chemicals. Could you, for instance, give away the printer with the purchase of a minimum amount of ink cartridges?

8. **Hourly Rates**—Nothing fancy here, you simply bill your jobs based on the amount of time it takes to complete each job.

9. **Licensing**—You get a fixed amount for a time period or unit sold. Sell your product to a large company with global distribution and receive a licensing fee or royalty on every unit sold. License your photos or other content for people to use on their blogs or websites. You can even license patents, processes, and business names.

10. **Upfront with Maintenance**—This method is extremely popular in the software industry. You pay a one-time fee for the software and then a percentage each year for maintenance and support.

These models are clearly not exhaustive, but our goal is to provide you with a good foundation to get your creative juices flowing, and to get you thinking about your revenue streams from a different vantage point. It is also important to note that most successful businesses utilize as many of these methods as possible to provide significantly more flexibility and diversity for their customers. You should constantly be on the lookout for opportunities to combine service trips or bundle product or service offerings, as this will allow you to make more money and deliver a product at an overall lower price to your consumer.

Question # 9: How Will You Scale Your Business?

Most businesses are initially exclusively dependent on their founders and key employees. In order to successfully scale your business, you will have to learn how to depend on processes, not people. This means documenting every job and every business process, while looking for ways to automate as many functions as possible. It also may mean outsourcing functions based on your new size and scale. For instance, you may have started an online business from your home, moved to a small warehouse, then a bigger warehouse, and now you might need several facilities to better serve your customers. Can you really afford all those facilities? Probably not, so you might decide to stock your inventory at a third party facility and have it handle your fulfillment needs. As a business owner, you will have to move from working in your business, to working on your business. If your business will not allow you to take a week or two off for a well-needed vacation, your business is not ready to scale.

You have to ask this simple question: Am I running my business or is my business running me? For most small business owners, the unfortunate answer is the latter. Many small business owners actually own jobs, not businesses. Once you have the infrastructure in place to scale your business, here are four ways to attack the market:

1. Sell more of your current products and services to existing customers.
2. Sell your current products and services to new customers.
3. Sell new products and services to existing customers.
4. Sell new products and services to new customers.

As we mentioned earlier in this chapter, opening a small business should really be viewed as a labor of love, and should be a decision made out of happiness. The true benefit to opening your own business is that you get to do so on your own terms. If you succeed, you have only you and your team to applaud. If you fail, you can only look in the mirror to see why. There is an exciting intersection where opportunity meets happiness, and for us, that is where we decided we wanted to lay our roots. Our journey to the specific type of business we opened began from a personal tragedy. But it was also that tragedy and that diagnosis that opened up our eyes to our absolute need for a better and higher quality of life.

This chapter should have provided you with a pretty strong argument to shift your personal paradigm when identifying whether or not you live a happy life, along with offering you some extremely useful resources and tools that can be used early on to determine exactly how you can create, and then build on, the momentum of your new business. In fact, this chapter may have asked you enough questions to push you to reconsider whether opening a small business would actually make you happy. That also would be a win for us. We found our own happiness. It is not for everyone, but it works for us. Most importantly, we want you to find that special happiness that can open the doors for a wildly successful opportunity, in one form or another.

Chapter 4
ACHIEVING YOUR DREAMS:
Ready to Go?

*T*here is a classic children's novel entitled *Harold and the Purple Crayon*, written by Crockett Johnson. The central character, Harold, is an inquisitive young boy who, with his purple crayon, has the power to create a world of his own just by drawing it.

Harold wants to go for a walk in the moonlight, but there is no moon, so he draws one. He has nowhere to walk, so he draws a path. He has many adventures on his journey—sailing, ballooning, picnicking, and even climbing a mountain to find his way home.

In a strange parallel, Harold was acting like any entrepreneur in that he had a need and created a solution. He thought outside of the box (Crayon box at least) and created his reality. Things don't always go as planned on his journey, but he creates a solution and redirects his efforts to ensure his success. In the end he is happy, fulfilled, and content.

If you're thinking about becoming an entrepreneur and starting your own business, be like Harold—grab your purple crayon and just get started. Oftentimes, beginning a project is the biggest hurdle we face. But once we get started, it's easy to keep going. A body in motion tends to stay in motion. A body at rest tends to stay at rest. The fastest way to achieve success in business is _"To BE in Business."_

This statement might not seem all that insightful on first read, but we are about to demonstrate to you just how profoundly true this is, and how it can totally change your life.

First, let us give you some insight: If you are waiting for that "perfect" business idea or plan to get started, you will likely never begin. Nothing is ever perfect, and there will always be an obstacle, concern, or fear just around the corner. Yes, the grass is always greener—and if you're always looking for the greener grass, you will never get started on fulfilling your dreams and achieving the happiness you desire. So if you haven't started yet, when you complete this book just choose an idea that is most aligned with your vision (it doesn't have to be perfect) and GET STARTED.

Only when _you are in business_ will you truly start to transform and grow, overcome your fears, and start to build your confidence. Only when you are in business will you start to receive real customer feedback you can build on, and see the next big thing, and the next big thing after that. Just as you cannot learn to swim without getting wet, you cannot succeed in business without being in business. You have to get started to make any real tangible progress.

A Lesson in Success

On the South Side of Chicago back in 1908, there lived a six-year-old boy and his widowed mother. Money was tight, so this boy (we'll call him William) got a job selling newspapers. William quickly learned that all the older kids had already secured the best corners for selling papers. When William tried to sell his papers anywhere near these high traffic corners, the older and bigger boys threatened him with beatings. But

William had already purchased a bundle of papers to resell, and if he could not find a way to sell them, he'd be out all his money. So what do you think he did? What would you have done if you were six and couldn't sell your papers on the prized corners?

You guessed it—he looked for a different location. Not a better corner, those were all taken. Instead, he remembered this restaurant he and his mom often walked past. It was called Hoelle's Restaurant, and it was always packed. For William, the thought of going inside on his own was more than a bit frightening, as he'd never been in a fancy restaurant. He was scared and nervous, so before he could talk himself out of it, he hurriedly walked inside and sold a paper to the very first table, and another at the second, and then yet another at the third. On his way to the fourth table, Mr. Hoelle grabbed William and quickly escorted him out the front door.

So what do you suppose William did? He gave up and went someplace else, right? Not a chance; he waited until Mr. Hoelle wasn't looking and walked right back in. The customer at the fourth table was so impressed with William's gumption that he not only paid for the paper, but also gave William an extra dime before Mr. Hoelle escorted William back out the door again.

Now, most six-year-olds would be satisfied with selling four papers and getting a tip. But not William, he walked right back in and started selling again. At this point, the entire restaurant was cheering for him, and when Mr. Hoelle tried to escort him back out the door, one of the customers said to let him be, which Mr. Hoelle did. About 5 minutes later, William had sold all of his papers.

The following night, William was back, and Mr. Hoelle was ready to kick him out of the restaurant once again. But just as quickly as Mr. Hoelle had escorted William out the door, William had entered again. Throwing up his hands, Mr. Hoelle said, "What's the use?" and let him sell his papers. Ultimately, the two became great friends.

So, who was William? William, it turns out, was Mr. W. Clement Stone. He would go on to turn a hundred dollar investment into several billion dollars, and donate nearly $275 million to charity over his lifetime.

What is it that you need to succeed? Certainly you need a goal, but you also need the same persistence and perseverance that W. Clement Stone displayed as a frightened but determined six-year-old boy. Stone once stated, *"Regardless of what you are or what you have been, you can still become what you may want to be."*

And that's not all we can learn from six-year-old William. His motivation was high because he and his mother needed the money. He'd already invested his pennies in buying the newspapers, and there was no refund for unsold papers.

William was afraid to enter the restaurant, but he pushed right through that fear before it could get the best of him. He knew going back into the restaurant after being thrown out might embarrass him, but he did it anyway because he was determined to sell those papers. William knew that achieving the goal was more important than the risk of being embarrassed.

He had the motivation and the determination to succeed, but perhaps most importantly, he had an amazing thought process that allowed him to find a new outlet for paper sales—it was almost impossible for him to fail. How you think matters, which means that how you think when you decide to launch your business really matters!

The Rubber Meets The Road

When it comes to your business and your life, a small vision will limit your potential, but a big vision will pull you toward more success than you believed possible. James Allen once said, *"You will become as small as your controlling desire; as great as your dominate aspiration."* The following tips will help you achieve your life's vision:

Your Big "Why"—William's big "why" was the simple need to help his mom put food on the table. You can start just about any business with a little creativity. But the first question you should be asking yourself is not what to start, but what you want to get out of your business. Do you want freedom? Do you want fame? Financial success? Do you want to make a difference? By knowing what you want, you'll be much more likely to push through the fear and be successful in figuring out how to obtain your goals. Let us give you an example: Let's say you are offered $100 to cross a 4 inch wide beam some 100 yards between two skyscrapers 1,000 feet in the air. If you are like us, your reaction would be a quick no, along with some additional adjectives not suitable for printing in this book. But let us change one variable—instead of $100, you need to cross the beam to save the single most important person in your life. In this case, your reaction is completely different and you will suppress the fear, take the risk, and cross the beam. What changed? Your "why" changed. If your "why" is big enough, you can achieve amazing things with your life. Know your "why," as it will motivate you through the setbacks and challenges you will surely encounter.

Your Value Proposition—No matter what field you are in, creating a value proposition for your business will allow you to clearly express how the benefits of your products or services translate into the value your customers will receive. We like to express our value propositions based on three key benefits: *better, faster,* and *cheaper.* If your proposed business cannot offer one or more of these three benefits, we suggest you seriously re-evaluate your plans. If the only box you can check is "better," you need to quickly validate that your customers are willing to pay for "better." Conversely, if you can check all three boxes, you likely have a winner on your hands. Your value proposition focuses on what your customers receive, not your technology or product features. Customers are focused on how you will make their lives better, save them money, or simply get things done faster.

Take Action—We've all had light bulb moments when a great idea popped into our head that, if pursued, could make us a lot of money, improve people's lives, or just plain solve an existing problem. But guess what? An idea isn't doing anything for anybody until action is taken! Without action, your life's vision and goals are merely dreams. Action is the fuel of success. As Bruce Lee said, *"If you spend too much time thinking about a thing, you'll never get it done."*

Think Without Fear—If action is the fuel of success, fear is the chain that holds us back from achieving our visions. One of the biggest obstacles people face is fear. Whether it's fear of starting a new business, building a new relationship, or starting a new job, fear will hold you back from realizing your life's vision. And if you allow fear to continually hold you back, you will have a life full of regrets.

To help overcome your apprehensions, we put together *The Top 3 Steps to Conquering any Fear:*

1. Write down the worst possible outcome that is creating your fear. There's something therapeutic about writing down what's creating all your worries. By writing down your fears, you are creating clarity and putting everything in perspective. Fears in the abstract tend to grow so big they can take over your life. But when you quantify your fears they become words on paper, and you can easily manage.

2. Decide you can deal with the worst possible outcome. Maybe your fear is that if you fail, you will lose everything financially. How would you deal with that? Probably by starting over and beginning again. Can you deal with that? You need to decide.

3. Work very hard to make sure the worst possible outcome does not happen. Decide what you need to do and then just do it. Nothing dispels fear faster than taking action.

Think Like A Bronze Medal Winner—A team of researchers found that while gold medalists are the happiest of all the Olympic competitors, bronze medalists are actually happier than the silver medalists.[23] So naturally we've got to ask ourselves—why are the people who come in third place happier than those who beat them and come in second?

The researchers believe this is caused by "counter factual thinking," or thinking about what might have been if only something had been different. The silver medalist might very well be thinking, "What if I had just gone ever so slightly faster? I would have won!" But the bronze medal winner might be thinking, "Wow, I almost didn't get a medal at all!"[24] It appears that silver medalists view themselves as the first loser, while bronze medalists think of themselves as the last winner.

This is top down thinking versus bottom up thinking, and it can make a vast difference in how you view yourself and your business. It can even determine how happy you allow yourself to be.

If you view your business as struggling and unsuccessful compared to those who appear more successful than you, you're more likely to be unhappy and dissatisfied. But if you actually compare your business to those that are smaller than yours, less successful, or struggling more, you're more likely to be happy. While we don't recommend you compare yourself to others, if you must, do it on a downward scale. This will actually put you in a better frame of mind to accomplish more.

Bottom line: If you want to achieve your life's gold medal, think like the bronze medal winner.

Focus on Progress—Most goals can be divided into smaller sequential steps. For instance, let's say you decided to launch a part-time business with the ultimate goal of quitting your day job. You might break this goal into 5 smaller steps such as:

- Get everything ready to start the business (knowledge, plan, funding, tools)

- Make $500/month from the business
- Make $1,000/month from the business
- Make $2,000/month from the business
- Make enough to quit your job and go full-time

We also recommend that you set a timeline for when you are going to achieve each one of the steps. By placing a date on which to achieve each step, you will ensure you stay focused and on track. Just don't pull a date out of the air; come up with a clear task list. Identify exactly what you need to do to complete each step. Try to figure out how long it will take to achieve each item on your list.

Your task list doesn't need to be long or complicated, but it should be clear. If any items are vague, then break them down further. Once your big goal has been divided into smaller manageable steps, you know what you need to do during the next week or two, and you can see the milestones mapped out for the next few months or years.

Recent studies have shown that the most effective goals are those we believe we have a 70% chance of achieving. At 70% we believe that our best effort is worthwhile and the end goal is actually attainable. Goals beyond 70% can seem unattainable and we will likely put little effort toward achieving our goals; below 70% you are not pushing yourself enough to achieve your best, so progress will be slow.

Establish Priorities—Would you turn down $500,000 for 1 hour of work? Richard Branson did! Here is the back story: *SUCCESS* magazine ran a cover feature with the knighted Sir Richard Branson, and shortly after the story they had a client contact them to inquire about hiring Branson to speak at their conference. Darren Hardy, the publisher of *SUCCESS* tells the story: "So, we had someone inquire and Sir Richard declined. The client then offered $250,000 for an hour talk, and again Sir Richard declined. They then raised it to $500,000, but Sir Richard still declined. Then we asked how much it would take to get Sir Richard to attend. The response from his people was, 'no amount of money would matter.' They said, 'Right now Richard has three main priorities he is focused on and he will only allocate his time to those three priorities, and speaking for a fee is not one of them.'"[25]

This is an extreme example of establishing priorities and staying committed. Determining the correct number of priorities for your maximum performance varies by individual, but almost always falls between three to five, with seven being really close to the maximum anyone can manage. Any more than three to five areas of focus ultimately results in no focus at all.

Critical Success Factors (CSFs)—Whatever business you are in, you need to have a detailed understanding of the business metrics that will lead to your success. As a business owner, there are so many priorities competing for your attention that it's often difficult to see the "forest for the trees." As a leader, if you are not driving the correct behaviors to ensure your business's success, how can you expect everyone on your team to be focusing on the true essentials? That's where Critical Success Factors come in. CSFs are the essential areas of activity that must be executed if you are to achieve business success. By identifying your Critical Success Factors, you can create a common point of focus for your business. As a common focal point, CSFs help everyone in the company know exactly what's most important. CSFs help people align their individual work with the overall metrics that will drive company success.

Like with priorities, we recommend you limit the number of CSFs to seven or fewer absolute essentials. By really focusing on your most critical CSFs, you can create maximum clarity, and ensure proper prioritization to other elements of your business. In reality, identifying your CSFs is an ongoing process. Your mission, strategic goals, and CSFs should all be linked and aligned to achieve success.

Let's take a look at the steps that will help you identify the CSFs for your business:

- ✓ <u>Step One:</u> Establish your business mission and strategic goals.
- ✓ <u>Step Two:</u> For each strategic goal, ask yourself, "What area of business is essential to achieve this goal?" The answers to the question are your candidate CSFs.
- ✓ <u>Step Three:</u> Evaluate the list of candidate CSFs to find the absolute essential elements for achieving success—these are your Critical Success Factors.
- ✓ <u>Step Four:</u> Identify how you will monitor and measure each of the CSFs.
- ✓ <u>Step Five:</u> Communicate your CSFs to employees.
- ✓ <u>Step Six:</u> Monitor, adjust, and update your CSFs to ensure you continue progressing towards your goals.

Modeling Your Business—For most business owners, the ultimate goal is to create a business that can be managed and run on a daily basis without them. Achieving this goal requires you to build systems and processes that will allow your business to scale. There are four key areas you will need to focus on to achieve this objective: 1) your economic model; 2) your lead generation system; 3) budgeting; 4) your human resource plan.

Your Economic Model: In simple terms, how will you make money? The four key elements to your economic model are: Sales, Cost of Goods Sold (COGS), Operating Expenses, and Net Income.

- <u>Sales:</u> The total amount of money that your business receives from selling goods or services.
- <u>Cost of Goods Sold:</u> The direct costs attributable to the production of the goods sold by your company. This includes

the cost of the materials used in creating the goods along with the direct labor costs used to produce the goods. It excludes indirect expenses such as distribution costs and sales force costs.

- Operating Expenses: A category of expenditure that your business incurs as a result of conducting its normal business operations. One of the typical responsibilities as a business owner is determining how to optimize operating expenses to maximize your ability to compete. Examples of these expenses include the payment of worker's wages, marketing, rent, and supplies.

- Net Income: The amount of profit your business earns, often referred to as "the bottom line" (since net income is listed at the bottom of the income statement). Net income is calculated by taking revenues and adjusting for the cost of doing business, depreciation, interest, taxes and other expenses.

Armed with an understanding of what drives your profit, you want to estimate when your business will break even. Start by forecasting your revenue for each of the next three years. Then do the same for your expenses. When will your revenue equal your expenses? By going through this quick exercise, you will be able to get a firm handle on your cash flow needs.

Lead Generation: Without customers, your business will not survive long. The process of obtaining prospects and customers is referred to as lead generation. Most marketing experts recommend companies use at least ten different lead generation methods to make sure the sales pipeline remains full. There are five critical elements to your lead generation system:

1. Building a Database
2. Feeding the Database

3. Contact Management
4. Conversion
5. Service

Let's say you get 100 people that come to your website and you are able to get 10 of those website visitors to give you their email address. With 10 people out of 100 opting in to your list, you have a 10% opt-in rate (10/100). Now you have 10 leads to whom you can market your product or service. Let's say you have 1 person out of the 10 who buys your product—you now have a 10% conversion rate (1/10). Given this scenario, if 100 people to come to your site, 10 people will opt-in and 1 of those will buy from you. If you want 10 customers, you need to send 1,000 people to your website. As a business owner, you will need to continually work to drive your opt-in and conversion rates higher. The higher your conversion rates, the more money you will make for the same lead generation spend.

To manage your lead generation activities and measure your results, you will need to enroll with a contact management service provider. There are very popular service providers online like AWeber, MailChimp, GetResponse, IContact, and Constant Contact.

You can get your lead generation efforts rolling and start building your email list by driving traffic to your website via Pay Per Click (PPC) advertising like Google Adwords, search engine optimization, forum and blog commenting, article writing, link building, blogging, joint ventures, YouTube, podcasting, Twitter, Facebook, and Pinterest. All of these will generate more qualified traffic for your business. If you want to learn more about lead generation, our book *Ultimate Marketing Hacks* comes with a free lead generation training guide.

Budgeting: The process of forecasting (and then matching) current and future revenue to expenses is known as budgeting. The goal is to make sure your cash flow is sufficient enough to keep your business growing. Without a budget, your business runs the risk of spending more money than you expected, or conversely, you risk not investing enough money to grow your business.

The chaotic nature of business revenue is one of the risks of being in a small business. The following tips will help you reduce the risks by creating a solid budget.

1. *Create Realistic Sales Projections*
   Your sales will likely trail your projection in your first months of operation, as it is very difficult to project sales in your early days of operation; your goal is to be as realistic in your projections as possible. It's certainly more prudent to underestimate your potential business income than to overestimate when you are initially setting up your budgets.

2. *Save Some Profits*
   It is sound business practice to keep some of your profits in reserve to cover any unexpected expenses. Even if you are operating a part-time business from home, do not withdraw all of your business profits each month. Instead, work out a reasonable withdrawal amount and pay yourself regularly, as part of the budgeted expenses of the business. If your sales are higher than you expect in one month, don't be tempted to splurge in the next month; instead, build some reserves or reinvest those funds to accelerate your business growth.

3. *Pay Off Debt Quickly*
   While it may be difficult to start your business without some debt, we recommend you eliminate your debt as soon as practical. Debt raises the cost of operating your business and could leave you in an uncompetitive market position. If you do take out a debt for your business, ensure you will be able to make the payments every month. When used properly, debt

can accelerate your business growth, but you want to make sure you have a strong degree of predictability in your sales and expenses to reduce the risks associated with adding leverage to your business.

Your Human Resource Plan—One of the most exciting moments in the life of your business is when you realize you need additional help to support your customers and continue to grow your business. When it's time to hire that first employee, you should really ask yourself if you should hire an employee or consider outsourcing the tasks via an online marketplace like Odesk or Elance.

If you don't have enough work to hire people and keep them working on a consistent schedule, it's usually better to outsource. Outsourcing allows you to match your individual needs with contractors who excel in those areas. Maybe you need help with accounting, web design, content creation, and marketing? You could outsource each of those tasks to four different contractors for say ten hours each week. Since it would be extremely difficult to find one person with all the various skills you need, outsourcing is a great solution.

Another option to consider is staffing agencies; they allow you to try employees without the typical headaches associated with conducting an expensive staffing search on your own. If you find the employee is not working out, you just call the staffing agency and they take care of everything for you. If the agency employee is doing a great job, most agency agreements allow you to convert your contractor to an employee after a period of time, typically at least ninety days.

Independent contractors are technically self-employed, which means you don't carry the burden of managing payroll, employment taxes, and the other obligations of managing employees. However, keep in mind that it is still your responsibility to ensure that you properly handle any potential tax or regulatory requirements involved with hiring independent contractors.

But before you rush off to find an outsource contractor or staffing agency, consider the following:

- Outsourced workers may not care as much about the work as an actual employee. Employee agencies likely have many clients and priorities, so you might find you're not receiving the best talent.
- Any information, trade secrets, business plans, etc., provided to an outsourced worker may be at risk. Screening potential agencies and understanding their legal responsibilities is a must, especially if they will be handling sensitive information.

Finally, certain tasks or jobs are just best left to experts. Legal services and information technology, for example, are often outsourced, as are accounting and bookkeeping. Customer service and administrative tasks, such as contact management, invoicing, and even inventory management, are other frequently outsourced tasks. When making a decision on whether to hire or outsource, ask yourself the following question: Is this task or job a core competency of our business? If the answer is no, then it is a likely candidate for outsourcing.

Where Did They Go Wrong?

We've all made some decisions in our lives that ultimately turned out to be bad choices. Sometimes we decide to do nothing, sometimes we pass on what later turns out to be an amazing deal, and sometimes we jump into things without thinking. The key thing to remember is that you are not alone, as chances are somebody has made a worse decision than you. With that said, let's take a look at some decisions that turned out to be quite bad. Through reviewing these examples of how one bad decision can lead to the inevitable collapse of an entire infrastructure, we are hopeful you will then see how important every decision can be towards the overall progress and prosperity of your business.

1. *Excite passes on Google*

   You likely are unfamiliar with Excite, but in the 1990s, Excite was one of the most recognized brands on the web. Google was a young company emerging from a research project by Larry Page and Sergey Brin when they were both PhD students at Stanford University in California. Fast forward a few years and Google is one of the most recognized brands in the history of the world. It turns out that Excite had the opportunity to purchase Google for the paltry price of only $750,000. To put things in perspective, the average price of a home in Silicon Valley now costs over 1 million dollars.[26] Still, Excite balked at the opportunity, and the rest is history. Today, Google is worth around $380 billion and Google's co-founders Larry Page and Sergey Brin are among the richest people in the world (they currently rank at 17 and 18 respectively, with $33.1 billion and $32.8 billion).[27] We wonder how disappointed the pair was when they lost out on that $750,000 payday?

   <u>Lesson Learned:</u> What might seem like a major setback can ultimately turn out to be the best thing that has ever happened to you.

2. *Kodak squanders opportunity*

   During most of the 20th century, Kodak was synonymous with photographic film, and in the mid seventies they had about 90% of the market in the United States. The company's tagline "Kodak moment" even entered pop culture as a way to describe a special moment that demanded to be recorded for history.

Despite having invented the core technology used in digital cameras, Kodak began to struggle financially in the late 1990s as the transition to digital photography took hold. Little known to most, Kodak also developed the technology that would ultimately become the cell phone. In the ultimate example of a "squandered opportunity," rather than take these technologies and run with them, the company's executives instead decided to sit on their hands because they saw the advancements as a significant threat to their existing profits. If Kodak had done things differently, they might be the Apple or Google of today.

Lesson Learned: Strive to constantly improve and grow. Think about the decisions that could actually put you out of business and respond to those issues before the competition does.

3. *Blockbuster Video passes on Netflix*
   Blockbuster Video was the dominant player in the home movie and video game rental industry via their video rental shops. In the late 80s, the technology existed to deliver movies to your home via your local cable company. Although there were many issues with storage, bandwidth, and set top boxes, it was the obvious direction the industry was moving. In those days, Blockbuster Video seemed as common as Starbucks is today. At its peak in 2004, Blockbuster had about 60,000 employees and over 9,000 stores.

   In the early 2000s, Blockbuster passed on the opportunity to buy Netflix for about $50 million. Today, Netflix has a market value of about $25 billion with some 50 million global subscribers, and over 30% market share in the United States' video streaming market.

   Blockbuster, on the other hand, kept doing what they were doing. They did finally introduce DVD-by-mail, streaming, and video on demand, but it was too little too late. Blockbuster filed for bankruptcy on September 23, 2010.[28] On April 6, 2011, the company and its remaining 1,700 stores were bought by satellite television provider Dish Network at an auction for $233 million.[29]

Lesson Learned: Embrace technology and focus on your customers. How can you deliver your product quicker, easier, and cheaper? Always strive to improve the customer experience before your competitor does.

4. *Ross Perot passes on Microsoft*

Henry Ross Perot is a billionaire businessman best known for being an independent presidential candidate in 1992 and 1996. Perot founded Electronic Data Systems (EDS) in 1962, sold the company to General Motors in 1984, and founded Perot Systems in 1988. Dell bought Perot Systems for $3.9 billion in 2009. With an estimated net worth of about $3.5 billion in 2012, Perot is ranked by *Forbes* as the 134th-richest person in the United States.[30]

By all accounts, Mr. Perot is one of the most successful businessmen of all time, but that does not mean he always got it right. In 1979, Perot negotiated with then 23-year-old Bill Gates to buy Microsoft for a price in the $50 million dollar range. Mr. Perot found that price to be out of the ballpark, so he passed. Bill Gates would go on to become the wealthiest person in the world, and Microsoft would become synonymous with modern computing.

"I should've just said, 'Now Bill, you set the price, and I'll take it,'" Perot said in an interview with *The Seattle Times* in 1992. "I should've just said, 'Bill, whatever you think is fair.'"

Lesson Learned: You can't get them all right! You will unquestionably miss some opportunities, but you can't harp on what is lost. If a billionaire like Ross Perot occasionally swings and misses, we can't expect to be perfect either.

Getting it Done

For every missed opportunity, bad decision, and failure to launch, history is filled with those who did get it right. One of the most unlikely success stories is Henry Ford, the founder of Ford Motor Company. Contrary to popular belief, Ford did not invent the automobile or the assembly line. Ford did, however, manufacture the first automobile that many middle class Americans could afford. In fact, many credit Ford for igniting the growth and wealth of middle class America. What you may not know is that Ford failed at his first two attempts to build an automobile company. The first time the company was dissolved. The second time he left because of disputes with his primary investor. It seemed that the automobile industry had completely written him off.

Yet, by 1914, Henry Ford had a much different problem: He was becoming too successful. Ford had introduced the moving assembly line at his Highland Park, MI plant in 1913, and it had worked far better than he could have imagined. The year before, he had doubled production of the Model T by doubling the size of his workforce. With the moving assembly line he nearly doubled production again, but this time he did it with the same number of workers. The assembly line had made production so efficient that the Highland Park payroll actually declined.

The problem Ford faced was that employee turnover was accelerating at an alarming rate. The mind-numbing work on the assembly line was causing workers to quit in droves.

Ford decided to take radical action. First, the company would reduce the workday from nine hours to eight. Second, it would move from two shifts a day to three shifts a day, opening up lots of new jobs. But the big news came in the third action: Ford would more than double the basic rate of pay to $5 a day. The company would spend an additional $10 million annually to improve productivity and the lives of its workers.

The "Five-Dollar Day" turned out to be an excellent investment. Within a year, annual labor turnover fell from 370% to 16%, and productivity rose from 40% to 70%. Between 1910 and 1919, Henry Ford reduced the Model T's price from around $800 to $350, solidified his position as the world's greatest automaker, and made himself a billionaire in the process.

<u>Lesson Learned:</u> Sometimes the solution to your problem requires an unconventional approach. With their pay doubled and hours reduced, Ford's employees were happy and more productive. With increased wealth and lower prices, a consumer revolution was begun. Too many companies look to long-term costs and cut programs that leave their employees feeling disenfranchised; sometimes the best solution is to share the wealth and create a bigger pie for everyone.

Another example of "getting it right" is found yet again in the car industry. When Toyota started shipping its first cars, Detroit was still concentrating on building powerful engines rather than raising overall quality. As new entrants, they offered smaller, cheaper, more fuel-efficient vehicles. Toyota's decision to put quality first wasn't as obvious as it might seem today, since at the time, the company was really struggling.

When Toyota entered the American market in the late 1950s, they were met with disdain for their shoddy quality. In fact, "Made in Japan" became synonymous with cheap and shoddy workmanship. In the midst of this crisis, President Taizo Ishida decided to adopt the ideas of an outsider—in this case the quality guru W. Edwards Deming, who turned the company upside down in order to improve it. Fast forward a few decades and Toyota became the largest automobile maker in the world. Today, manufacturers, distributors and even service companies around the world have adopted the Toyota quality system, known as the "Toyota Way."

As described by external observers of Toyota, the principles of the "Toyota Way" are:[31]

1. Base your management decisions on a long-term philosophy, even at the expense of short-term goals.
2. Create continuous process flow to bring problems to the surface.
3. Use "pull" systems to avoid overproduction.
4. Level out the workload.
5. Build a culture of stopping to fix problems, and focus on getting quality right the first time.
6. Standardized tasks are the foundation for continuous improvement and employee empowerment.
7. Use visual control so no problems are hidden.
8. Use only reliable, thoroughly tested technology that serves your people and processes.
9. Grow leaders who thoroughly understand the work, live the philosophy, and teach it to others.
10. Develop exceptional people and teams who follow your company's philosophy.
11. Respect your extended network of partners and suppliers by challenging them and helping them improve.
12. Go and see for yourself in order to thoroughly understand the situation.
13. Make decisions slowly by consensus, thoroughly considering all options; implement decisions rapidly.
14. Become a learning organization through relentless reflection and continuous improvement.

Lesson Learned: Toyota knew they needed a long-term solution to address consumer concerns, yet they did not respond with a marketing campaign or chase the latest trends and fads. Toyota looked far down the road and sought to develop the best cars that would last for a very long time. Sometimes the journey is long, but if you stick with it, great things can happen.

Ready to Go?

As this chapter has shown, there are a lot of variables to consider when starting your own business. Achieving your dreams requires a grand vision and a lot of hard work. Once you have established your big "why," you can determine your value proposition and take action. Remember that the only way to succeed in business is to BE IN business! There will be obstacles and you will experience fear, but with the help of this chapter, you can overcome even the worst possible scenario. By focusing on progress and establishing priorities and CSFs, you will position yourself for success. Our hope is that you can use this chapter, and the accompanying "Checklist for Starting Your Business" found in Appendix A, to help you successfully start your dream business. Feel free to return to this chapter as much as is needed when getting started. We worked hard and overcame many obstacles when starting our business, and we believe that the information contained in this chapter will be beneficial. Hopefully it will help you avoid some of the challenges we encountered. We want to help you get it done, and more importantly, we want to help you get it done right. So, are you ready to start achieving your dreams?

Chapter 5

THE TREASURE HUNT:
Building Your Business

*B*efore you can begin selling the goods, you have to acquire them! This chapter will help to educate you on the ins and outs of garage sales, flea markets, and other potential treasure troves. The first step in any shopping spree is planning the course, agreeing on a budget, and then making the most of the money you have in hand. There will surely be misses, but our goal will be to help you to identify the highest value items that can create the largest profit margins for you and your newly formed business.

The Treasure Troves
When looking for places to discover items to purchase and resell for a profit, there is a myriad of venues for you to explore. It is important you gain an understanding of the different types of venues available because we will be applying different strategies based not only on these types of sales outlets, but also on the seasons of the year.

Estate Sales

An estate sale is a sale or auction intended to dispose of all, or a substantial portion of, the property and/or belongings owned by a person who is recently deceased, or who must dispose of his or her personal property to facilitate a move.

The most common reason for an estate sale is the death of the property owner, and the consequent need to quickly liquidate the deceased's belongings. The survivors may have no interest in the bulk of the personal belongings left by the deceased, or may simply lack space to keep the belongings. In situations in which the survivors cannot agree to the disposition of tangible property, a court may order the goods to be sold in an estate sale with the proceeds to be divided among the survivors. Such a sale and division may also be mandated in the will of the deceased.

An estate sale may also occur because the property owner will be moving or has moved into a situation where he will be unable to keep his property—for example, a move to an assisted living facility, a retirement community, a rest home, or other living quarters.

An estate sale may also take place because of divorce, foreclosure, or relocation. In many regions hit hard by the foreclosure crisis, property owners are electing to liquidate their possessions. Often times these individuals are forced to move to an apartment or family member's residence.

Professional estate sale companies typically hold estate sales. The typical fees earned by estate sale companies' range from 25% to 40% of the estate sale revenues. This fee typically covers all costs, including advertising, marketing, research, labor, security, and other fees incurred to conduct a successful estate sale.

Estate sales are becoming more popular as our society has become more mobile. The use of professional estate liquidation companies is becoming a preferred process to reduce stress and potential conflict among family members. In addition, most estate liquidators have a consistent following of buyers including dealers, pickers, collectors and the general public. This base allows top liquidators to be familiar with buyer trends, and they have often built reputations for fair pricing, specialized knowledge, and experience.

Garage Sales

A garage sale or yard sale is an informal, occasionally scheduled event for the sale of property owned by private individuals. These sales are typically held in individuals' garages, yards, driveways, carports, or neighborhood community centers. Popular reasons that people conduct a garage sale include spring-cleaning, moving, or just a need for a little extra money.

Before conducting your own garage sale, check with your local officials to see if you are required to obtain a permit, or face any special requirements such as allowable hours, sale days, parking requirements, etc. Some cities, such as Beverly Hills, California, Gettysburg, Pennsylvania, Sweden, New York and Bessemer City, North Carolina require that the homeowners apply and pay for a garage sale permit. Even with a permit, homeowners in Beverly Hills can only hold yard sales in the back of their homes! Make sure your city doesn't have any strange stipulations regarding garage sales.

You can find all kinds of items at garage sales, but the most common items at sales include clothing, toys, art, books, household knickknacks, jewelry, fashion accessories, lawn and garden tools, and sports equipment. Garage sales occur most frequently in suburban neighborhoods on weekends during warm weather months. In many parts of the country, especially the Midwest, it is not unusual for sales to occur Thursday through Sunday.

Here in the United States, going to garage sales has spawned the use of a new verb—"garage saling." If you are going to multiple garage sales in one day, you are said to be "garage saling." The pun "garage fail" has also emerged to label a garage sale that is not worth going to. We hope you enjoy garage saling, and avoid garage fails.

Community Sales

In some areas, garage sales have taken on a special meaning to the community and have become events of special local significance. In these situations, large areas of a community hold a communal garage sale involving dozens or hundreds of families at the same time. These community sales are often great sources of products to sell online. Also, the fact that you can shop multiple sales all in the same location makes these sales very attractive. A few of these sales have become events that rival festival status.

The Highway 127 Corridor Sale is promoted as "The World's Longest Yard Sale." Private individuals and professional vendors conduct simultaneous yard sales along a 630-mile (1,010 km) corridor spanning five U.S. states.

Running east to west, the Coast-to-Coast yard sale runs along US-50 in May of each year. Though not as popular as "The World's Longest Yard Sale," the US-50 Coast-to-Coast sale is over a decade old.

During the second Saturday in August, a 50-mile stretch of U.S. Route 11 becomes a continuous yard sale that runs from Stephens City, Virginia's Newtown Commons, all the way south to New Market, Virginia. The Shenandoah County Chamber Advisory Group, five chambers of commerce, and two town governments sponsor the event.

Be sure to check your local newspaper for listings of community sales.

Flea Markets

A flea market or swap meet is a type of bazaar that rents space to people who want to sell or barter merchandise. The vendors at these events vary as greatly as the merchandise itself. While some venues focus on low priced items, many offer a wide array of bargain priced items.

The location of these venues varies, and many are located indoors in old grocery stores, warehouse buildings, or even in school gymnasiums. The larger venues are outdoors and cover acres of land. When it comes to flea markets and swap meets, there really are no consistent rules; many are held annually or semiannually, others may be conducted monthly, on weekends, or daily. Flea market vendors themselves take many forms. They vary from your local family that is renting a table for the first time to sell a few unwanted household items, to professionals who travel the area buying items from a multitude of sources.

Flea market vending, though similar in structure, should not be compared with street vending. The correlation between the two, though existent, is not exact. Flea market vending, as we know it, presents distinct elements setting it apart from street vending. Street vending takes place where a large crowd gathers and relies specifically on impulse buyers who are in the area at the time for underlying reasons. The flea market, however, is the arena and the vendors are the show that attracts the crowds that gather for the sole purpose of buying. Flea market vending is also set in a controlled area that is governed by a self-imposed code of conduct.

Charity Stores or Thrift Shops

Many local charitable organizations, both religious and secular, operate thrift shops. Common among these are missions, children's homes, homeless shelters, and animal shelters. In addition, some charity shops are operated by churches, and act as fundraising venues that support local church events and missionary activities in other countries.

These organizations typically sell used goods donated by members of the local community, and in most cases are staffed by volunteers with one or two paid employees. Because the items for sale are typically donated and operating costs are low, items can be sold at extremely low prices. In fact, thrift store merchandise is priced 50-75% below the original retail price, offering significant opportunities for you to purchase merchandise that can be resold for nice profits online. Charity shops sell a mix of clothing, books, music, and typical household items. Some shops specialize in certain areas like vintage clothing, furniture, electrical items, or records.

When you start out, it is a good idea to focus on the charity based thrift shops (my favorites are Goodwill and Savers). Shops like these have most of their merchandise donated, so their prices are typically low. It is not worth their time and energy to price each and every golf club that comes in the door, so they sell them at $2.98 each or some similar number. That means that an $80 driver is priced at $2.98 and a $1 driver is priced at $2.98—it is your job to know the difference.

Many of your local thrift shops are profit driven. They buy items at storage auctions, liquidation events, and even local yard sales. They offer what I call eBay pricing—the price you could buy the item for on eBay. This is a great deal compared to full retail, but since we will be selling on eBay we have to buy our items at a much better price point. The good news is that even these stores miss-price items, lump like items together, or simply don't understand what they have. This happens for a variety of reasons, which are typically related to a lack of resources and time. Before buying from these shops, visit your local stores, compare prices, look things up on eBay, and get a feel for each shop's approach to the market.

Classified Sites

Classified advertising is a form of advertising that is particularly common in newspapers and in various other periodicals, which may be sold or distributed, free of charge. Advertisements in a newspaper are typically short, as they are paid for by the line, and are only one newspaper column wide. Publications printing news or other information often have sections of classified advertisements; there are also publications that contain only advertisements. The advertisements are grouped into categories or classes such as "for sale—cars," "wanted—boats," and "services—plumbing," hence the term classified.

Classified advertisements are much cheaper than larger display advertisements used by businesses, and are mostly placed by private individuals with single items they wish to sell or buy. They can be a great source of merchandise for your business.

Like most forms of printed media, the classified ad has found its way to the Internet.

Internet classified ads do not typically use per-line pricing models, so they tend to be longer than printed ads. They are also searchable (unlike printed material), tend to be local, and may foster a greater sense of urgency as a result of their daily publication and wider scope for audiences. Due to their low cost structures and alternative monetization models, many companies offer free or near free listings.

A growing number of sites and companies have begun to provide specialized classified marketplaces online that cater to niche market products and services such as boats, pianos, pets, and adult services, amongst others. In many cases, these specialized services provide better and more targeted search capabilities than general search engines or general classified services can provide.

Craigslist.org is a classified advertisements website with sections devoted to jobs, housing, personals, general for sale, items wanted, services, community, gigs, and forums. Craig Newmark began the service in 1995 as an email distribution list for friends that featured local events in the San Francisco Bay Area. In 1996 it became a web-based service and expanded into other classified categories. It started expanding to other U.S. cities in 2000, and currently covers 50 countries and is one of the world's top 50 Internet sites. In recent years, bartering has exploded on Craigslist, and this site provides you an opportunity to trade items of value for items of greater use, broader market appeal, or just plain increased value. There have been many stories where individuals started with everyday household items and through a number of trades, converted these low dollar items into items worth thousands of dollars.

Craigslist is great for large, bulky, and heavy items where local pick up is the only viable option. Although eBay allows a local pick-up only option, you will still get emails from buyers wanting to know if you will ship to them if they pay shipping. Responding to these emails can become a big time waster, as eBay rates you on your responsiveness. For example, I recently got a quote to ship one of those water filled punching bags used in karate for $210 bucks; but the thing could be bought in your local store for $129! I still use eBay local pickup in conjunction with Craigslist, but it is important that you write your listing in a way that reduces or eliminates these types of time wasters.

Online Marketplaces

Online shopping or online retailing is a form of electronic commerce whereby consumers directly buy goods or services from a seller over the Internet. An online shop evokes the physical analogy of buying products or services at a brick-and-mortar retailer or shopping center. The process is called business-to-consumer (B2C) online shopping. When a business buys from another business it is called business-to-business (B2B) online shopping. The largest online retailing corporations are eBay.com and Amazon.com. Both eBay and Amazon will be significant outlets for your merchandise sales. These websites allow you to list individual items for sale, as well as create and maintain online shops, without the complexity and costs involved in developing your own e-commerce website.

Discount Stores

A discount store is a type of store that sells products at prices lower than those asked by traditional retail outlets. Most discount stores offer a wide assortment of goods; others specialize in merchandise such as jewelry, electronic equipment, or electrical appliances. Discount stores are not variety stores, which sell goods at a single price-point or multiples thereof. Discount stores differ from variety stores in that they sell many name-brand products and offer a wide price range on items. Following World War II, a number of retail establishments in the U.S. began to pursue a high-volume, low-profit-margin strategy designed to attract price-conscious consumers.

Going out of Business Sales

Regardless of the underlining economy, businesses go out of business every year. According to the Small Business Administration, about two-thirds (or 66 percent) survive longer two years, leaving a third of businesses that fail within these two years. Extended to four years, the number of surviving businesses decreases to only 44 percent, meaning that about 56 percent of businesses fail at the five-year mark.[32]

Growing up as a teen in Myrtle Beach, SC, I remember the beachwear shops that would conduct a "going out of business sale" at the end of every season. Which begs the question, when is a sale not a sale? How long can a "going out of business sale" last before a business closes its door? A month, a year, two years, longer? When the local community officials came down on these guys, signs went up that said "Going Out for Business Sale!" It took a while for people to catch on to this one, as our brains use heuristics or "short-cuts" and naturally read these clever signs as going *out* of business.

Of course, Myrtle Beach was not the only place to use these creative tricks, and many states now have statutes regulating going out of business sales. The owner of the business may be required to obtain a license and post a security bond to protect creditors and customers before conducting such a sale. A statement verifying the discontinuation of the business may also be required to prevent fraudulent advertising practices.

With that said, going out of business sales can be wonderful places to pick up not only merchandise, but also office equipment, furniture, display cases, shelving units, clothing racks, and so much more. You often can buy lots of new inventory in bulk, or lots of shelf pulls (new items out on the floor or display cases). It is important to keep in mind that wholesale liquidators will only pay 10 to 30 percent of original wholesale costs, so negotiate with this information in hand. By buying in larger quantities, you increase your odds of getting the best merchandise. Business owners will often try to bundle slow moving or low value items with their most desirable product in order to move the most product.

Sell Before You Buy—Local Markets

Most large cities have an area where importers sell large and small quantities of products at wholesale prices. In Houston it's Harwin Street, in New York it's Canal Street, in Chicago there are a few spots around downtown. Regardless of location, you can identify inventory sources and use Amazon and eBay to identify products you can sell for a profit. You can take digital photos and list these items on line. If they sell, you purchase the items and ship them off. However, you do need to ensure your vendors have an ample supply of inventory, as you do not want to get caught not being able to deliver your merchandise. Yes, you can cancel your auctions or sales and refund your buyers' money, but this will have a negative impact on your seller ratings. Still, if you are really tight on cash, this little known selling method gets you in the game.

Drop Shipping

Drop shipping is an inventory technique in which the seller does not keep goods in stock, but instead transfers customer orders and shipment details to either the manufacturer or a wholesaler, who then ships the goods directly to the customer. As in retail businesses, the majority of sellers make their profit on the difference between the wholesale and retail price, but some sellers earn an agreed percentage of the sales in commission, paid by the wholesaler to the seller.

Sellers that drop ship merchandise from wholesalers may take measures to hide this fact in order to avoid any stigma, or to keep the wholesale source from becoming widely known. Achieve this by "blind shipping" (shipping merchandise without a return address), or "private label shipping" (having merchandise shipped from the wholesaler with a return address customized to the seller). A wholesaler may introduce a customized packing slip to include the seller's company name, logo, and/or contact information.

Many sellers on online auction sites, such as eBay and Amazon, also drop ship. Often, a seller will list an item as new and ship the item directly from the retailer or wholesaler to the highest bidder. The seller profits from the difference between the winning bid and the wholesale price, minus any selling and merchant fees from the auction site.

Two significant benefits of drop shipping are the elimination of upfront inventory and a positive cash-flow cycle. A positive cash flow cycle occurs because the seller is paid when the purchase is made. The seller usually pays the wholesaler by credit card or credit terms. Therefore, there is a period of time in which the seller has the customer's money, but has not yet paid the wholesaler.

As in any business, some risks are involved in drop shipping. For example, backordering may occur when a seller places a shipment request with a wholesaler, but the product is sold out. Backordering may be accompanied by a long wait for a shipment while the wholesaler waits for new products, which may reflect badly on the seller. A good wholesaler will keep sellers updated, but it is the seller's job to be aware of the quantities that the wholesaler has available. Additionally, many drop shippers charge fees for small orders or have minimum dollar order levels. These fees can make selling low cost items impractical, or can force you to push these fees on to your end consumer thereby potentially pricing you out of the market.

Drop shipping has also featured prominently in some Internet-based home business scams.[33] Scam artists will promote drop shipping as a lucrative "work from home opportunity." The victim who buys into this scam will be sold a list of businesses from which drop-shipment orders can be placed. These businesses may not be wholesalers, but other businesses or individuals acting as middlemen between retailers and wholesalers, with no product of their own to sell. These middlemen often charge prices that leave little profit margin for the victim, and require a regular fee for the retailer's usage of their services. Be wary of these types of "opportunities." When in doubt, do some research.

Drop shipping on eBay does present some challenges. As a seller, you must guarantee your items are shipped within 30 days after the buyer's date of purchase, and you must state this guarantee in your listing. You must also state that the items for drop shipping are "pre-sale items," and the text of this advisory must be prominent, and not be smaller than HTML font size 3. The penalties for violating eBay pre-sale policies can be significant and include: Listing cancellation, limits on account privileges, account suspension, forfeit of eBay fees on cancelled listings, and loss of seller status like Top Rated, Power Seller, etc.

Due to the risks of utilizing drop shipping on eBay, we recommend you setup your own e-commerce site to implement this particular strategy.

Plotting the Course

If you want to be successful, you have to be smart about where and how to spend your time. Although shopping is fun, you must remember you are running a business, and with any business you simply have to have a plan of attack. Without proper planning, you will find you have wasted lots of your time and gas money driving all over town (or state), only to discover low-value, over-priced items.

When approaching your garage sale schedules, it is important to think about the residents of the homes you will be visiting. For instance, families with young children tend to gravitate to areas with the best school districts, singles tend to gravitate close to entertainment and shopping hubs, and young professionals gravitate to similar areas. Likewise, many older residential neighborhoods have owners who are elderly and who have been in their homes for decades.

Get to know the demographics of the neighborhoods in your area. What are the average home prices? Which communities are gated, have country clubs, and have the best schools? The odds of you finding higher end items in expensive neighborhoods are statistically more probable than in lower income neighborhoods. Is this the case 100% of the time? Of course not, but the odds are in your favor if you follow the money.

The first step to success is to understand your market, as this not only increases your odds for profit, but also helps you sequence the sales you will attend to maximize your results and minimize your effort and time.

In the Chicago market for instance, the Northwest suburbs are one of my favorite places to attend sales. Not only are the demographics extremely favorable, but also this Chicago area was a hub of manufacturing and an early cultural center in the United States throughout most of the 18th and early 19th century. This means I find a lot of niche items that have high resale value.

If you are located in a large city, it may be impractical for you to drive to all of the neighborhoods, and many mixed-use areas may be difficult to access with quick trips. If you find yourself in this situation, we recommend websites like www.city-data.com to quickly get the lay of the land. City Data has collected and analyzed data from numerous sources to create profiles of most U.S. cities, and it is free to use. They have the latest real estate prices and sales trends, recent home sales, hundreds of thousands of maps, satellite photos, stats about residents (race, income, ancestries, education, employment), geographical data, state profiles, crime data, registered sex offenders, cost of living, and much more. If you ever need to research any city, zip code, or neighborhood for any reason, this is a great place to start.

Jack-of-All-Trades, Master of None

There are three distinct paths people take when developing their businesses: 1) the specialization approach, 2) the general approach, and 3) the hybrid approach. Each approach has it strengths and weaknesses, so the key is to find a model that is best suited for your interests and lifestyle.

The specialization business model allows you to develop expert knowledge in your particular niche, and this knowledge can often lead to larger profits. As an example, let's say you have collected Barbie dolls ever since you were a little kid. You love Barbie dolls and know way more than you care to admit about them! You know the dolls that were special editions, the clothing and accessories, you know the ones that were hard to get, and you even know the dolls that were in big demand.

Armed with all your Barbie expertise, you would have no problem honing in on those rare and valuable dolls and accessories piled in the box at the neighborhood garage sale. Unlike the average person who will likely see just old kid's toys, you will be able to spot the potential diamonds in the ruff. If you specialize in Barbie dolls, you will build a client list of Barbie collectors and you will likely know exactly whom you will sell a particular doll to even before you have bought it! You may even become a go-to person for Barbie collectors, buyers, and reporters.

However, on the flip side of the equation, you may have limited opportunities to acquire Barbie dolls in your local market. You can attend many garage sales and flea markets and not come across a single Barbie doll. You can spend hours on eBay and Amazon looking for Barbie dolls that you can purchase and resell for a profit, but will there be enough of a supply to scale your business to the size you desire? Maybe you decide to expand your specialization to all dolls or dolls of a particular time frame, building on your Barbie expertise to expand your business opportunities.

When looking for areas of specialization, your hobbies and interests are a great place to start, but they are not the only place. Certain regions of the country are known for particular industries or a unique cultural significance. For instance, pottery was extremely popular in Chicago, and companies like Red Wing have pieces that are readily found at sales in the region. These items are quite scarce in other parts of the country, and I can often buy these items from $1 to $10 and sell them for 40, 50, or even 100 times my purchase price. Other regions of the country are known for jewelry making, hand carved toys, automotive products, farming equipment, or civil war relics. Learning about the history of your area and educating yourself on the products originating within your region can lead to large dividends.

The thing to remember when specializing is to ensure you define your niche in a way that will allow you to achieve your ultimate vision. The classic business school example is that of the buggy and buggy whip companies that failed to adjust to the consumer adoption of the automobile. Though similar products are still manufactured for limited purposes today, the buggy industry as a major economic entity ceased to exist with the introduction of the automobile. Companies that would have defined their niche slightly different, say transportation or transportation accessories, would have fared much better.

Many people starting out have trouble picking a particular niche, so they decide to become like a mini eBay themselves, buying and selling any items they think they can make a profit on. They may sell car mats, books, DVDs, or housewares. In fact, one of the things we recommend is to take various unwanted items from around your house that you no longer need and list them on eBay. You can quickly get a feel for the types of items people buy.

It might shock you to learn that people buy things like pine cones and empty toilet paper rolls on eBay! That's right, you can get about .18 cents each for those empty toilet paper rolls you have been throwing away for years! Schoolteachers, camps, day cares, and parents use them for arts and craft projects and are constantly looking for bundles of 50 or 100 empty roles. In fact, the last time we listed empty toilet paper rolls, they sold in less than two hours! We did not sell them because we are in the toilet paper niche; we did it simply to demonstrate that opportunities exist everywhere. If you live in the Southeast, pinecones may be a nuisance in your yard, but people in other parts of the country need to buy them for their craft projects. Get creative and look for opportunities!

When selling everything from A to Z, you introduce additional challenges like lack of expertise, uniform product storage, stocking various size boxes, and figuring out how to market to the various different consumer segments. It also becomes difficult to keep up with all the trends in the marketplace and with shifting consumer preferences. Most people develop a hybrid model where instead of focusing on a single product line, they elect to sell to a broad category like fashion. They may focus on items from particular brands, like Coach, Michael Kors, or Kate Spade, knowing they can gain expertise and synergies around both the product and their customers.

The sky is really the limit when it comes to what you can buy and resell for a profit. We have broken down the market into 18 specific categories for simplification purposes. The categories can be greatly expanded and many sub categories can be developed. Our goal here is to get you thinking about the opportunities available and provide you with some ideas to get you started. Pick an area where you have an interest and start building your knowledge base:

1. Advertising collectibles
2. Architecture
3. Art
4. Books, magazines, and paper
5. Clothing, fabric, textiles
6. Coins, currency, stamps
7. Film and television
8. Glass and pottery
9. Household
10. Kitchen collectibles
11. Memorabilia
12. Music
13. Nature and animals
14. Sports
15. Technology
16. Themes
17. Toys, games, dolls
18. Fitness Equipment

You can also use Appendix B, "Ideas For Items You Can Buy and Resell," at the end of the chapter for additional ideas.

The Do's and Don'ts of Buying

In real estate it is all about location, location, location! When finding the best deals, it is all about timing, timing, timing! Although there may be no hard and fast rules for all types of sales, the general rules to remember are "the earlier the better" and "later can be greater!"

When shopping estate sales for instance, there are typically two best times to find deals. The first is the opening of the sale on the first day and the next is on the last day of the sale. During the first day you want to get to the sale 30 minutes to an hour prior to the sale start. Many sales restrict the number of people in the home at any given time, and will actually use a number system to control access.

You want to be in the first group through the house to ensure you have the first chance at the best items, and perhaps discover valuable items that may not have been recognized by the estate sale representatives. Common mispriced items include artwork, collectibles, toys, and vintage items. Most prices will be marked and the estate sellers will typically hold firm on pricing during the first day. On the last day, most items are 50% off and as the day comes to a close, prices become very flexible.

Some estate sale companies will move items from sale to sale or list unsold items online, but most of the estate sale companies recognize that if an item did not move in the first sale, it is better left behind for donation. Exceptions are typically expensive pieces of furniture, art, or jewelry that would sell better in an auction setting.

Since most estate sale companies typically group like items, it is important you take a quick pass of all the rooms. Collectibles tend to be aggregated in the main home area, while kid's stuff—toys, posters, clothing, etc.—tends to remain in the bedrooms. Homes with basements tend to aggregate a lot of old stuff—vintage toys, the old camera collections, sporting equipment, artwork, and other items of value. We often find more items of value in the basement than in any other location in the home. This is not only because the old stuff seems to end up there, but also because the nature of the clutter and storage often makes it more difficult for estate sale companies to properly value these items.

A typical estate sale company will spend 3 to 5 days organizing and pricing items for the weekend sale. Most companies rely on friends, family, and part-time workers to prepare the house. The pure logistics in conducting the actual sale event virtually ensure there is little chance that all items are properly priced. In fact, many items worth hundreds of dollars are often tagged at less than $5 or $10 bucks. This is especially true with items like art, toys, vases, jugs, purses, and jewelry.

Quite often, valuable items get lumped in with the common items, as nobody is an expert across all categories and individual products. In fact, poor lighting can easily lead to a maker's mark being missed, a signature print being placed in the poster pile, or a diamond ring being mixed in with the costume stuff. As mentioned earlier, we once found a vintage autographed blues festival poster worth thousands that was lumped in with some everyday kid's wall posters. We have found diamond rings, expensive watches, collectibles, designer handbags, and much more just thrown in with other items of little value.

Best Time to Shop Moving Sales

Moving sales are fantastic opportunities to purchase larger items that you can sell on Craigslist and at local festivals and shows. On more than one occasion, we have been offered an item in return for simply removing it from someone's home.

In addition, most homes have heavy and fragile items that are very expensive to move, and this can mean opportunity for you. Moving sales are a bit unique as people often plan to hold the sale across several different weekends. They may start with a traditional garage sale to downsize items that they no longer need. We find that patio, lawn, and garden equipment go first when people are moving from homes to condos or downsizing all together. It is important to build a relationship with the sellers and learn their plans for selling their items.

Moving sales typically occur at least twice in the process; the first weekend people are trying to get as much as possible for their items, so during this weekend we will use different buying strategies to ensure we are getting the best deals possible. The next phase for most movers is what I call the "Just Get Rid Of it Day." At this point the sellers are tired, frustrated, and ready to move on. The natural reaction of the majority of buyers is to skip the sale all together. They recognize the house, have already attended the sale, and believe everything left must be junk. In most cases they are right, but there are times where they are wrong enough to make this day worth your while.

Everybody has emotional attachment to items ranging in value from small to significant, and even though they are attached, they still know they must sell (even if they do not want to). Often times, they have been holding on to these items wanting to get top dollar in order to make the sale a little less emotional. You want to learn about these items in your earlier visits. Sellers will tell you a story about the item, how they purchased it on a vacation, anniversary, for their first home, etcetera. In some cases, items may have even been given a name by their owners, which is often the case with a lot of cars. In this event, you will have an asking price that reflects this emotional attachment. You want to note these items in your journal or smart phone, along with the story attached to the items and the asking price.

Your strategy at this point is to simply work on building a relationship with the sellers. Avoid making a low ball offer too early, as many others will do this. When you do return, you can note how surprised you are that the beautiful keepsake they bought on their anniversary in Hawaii is still available. They will tell you how surprised they are as well, and how many insulting offers they received on their particular cherished treasures. At this point, you want to let them talk as much as possible. You then want to tell them how much you love the item and that you understand why they are reluctant to sell. You do not want to insult them, but you can explain that you are on an extremely tight budget, and ask for the best selling price they are willing to offer. Make sure to reassure them that the item will have a wonderful home. I cannot tell you the number of times we get an item for a price less than what they have already turned down as an insult by prior buyers. This simple change of dynamic makes all the difference in the world to the seller.

The fact is, any money they receive for their cherished item will never exceed their emotional attachment, but you have given them something more—a story they can tell about the person who loved the item almost as much as they did and how happy they are the item found a great home. Understanding the landscape, building a relationship, and creating a shared experience can give you an unmatched advantage when dealing with emotional sellers. We are not suggesting you be disingenuous in your approach; we are just demonstrating to you the power of building connection and understanding the goals and objectives of sellers. Even veterans of sales often get so focused on particular items that they forget the items are bought and sold by human beings; people will always give better deals to those they like or feel an affinity with.

Most people enjoy getting out and attending sales on a beautiful day, but bad weather means opportunity. Bad weather simply keeps most people away. As an experienced buyer, you will learn to love the bad weather, as it represents a major opportunity due to the sheer number of people staying home. The more people staying at home not only translate to less competition, but also to more negotiating power, especially at estate sales. These companies need to finish the sale on schedule and in almost all cases, must finish due to contract and scheduling commitments. Can you say opportunity?

Best Time to Shop Thrift Stores

When you are new to buying from thrift stores, we recommended you visit the charity-based stores first; however, there are actually better times of the month to shop at your profit-based thrift stores as well. Most of these shops will negotiate more toward the end of the month, and in the first few days of the current month as they face rent and other expenses for both their shop and personal lives. The inventory won't pay the bills while taking up space on their shelves, so they need to convert it to cash.

Know Your Numbers

Just like the sellers you are buying from, you have a budget you need to develop and manage. Knowing your numbers is necessary to the success of your business. How much money can you comfortably spend to build inventory each month? How long does it take to sell or turn your inventory? What price points sell the best on eBay? How much time do you need to take photos, list items, and ship your product? How much inventory do you need listed to achieve your desired income levels?

We have found that selling items around $60 to $80 creates the most profit for us. At this price point, there are lots of buyers who can afford your prices, and the return on your time and money is optimized. A key point for you to understand is that it generally takes as much time to list a $10 item as it does an $80 item. Unless your items are standardized, easy to list, and inexpensive to ship, like books or CDs, we do not recommend you buy items that list for under $20. There are lots of household, collectibles, fashion, vintage, and other items you can buy for under $15 or $20 that will sell for $60 to $80, or even more. Don't forget your time needs to be budgeted and managed as well. You want to ensure you maximize not only the return on your purchase price, but also the return on your time.

Seek and You Shall Find

You now have a working knowledge of the treasure troves available to help make you some money! You can find high profit, resalable products at estate sales, garage sales, community sales, flea markets, thrift shops, classified sites, online markets, and discount stores. You can also get to know your local markets and visit "Going Out of Business" sales. In addition, you can choose to sell before you buy, and utilize drop shipping. With all of those options, planning and scheduling are of the utmost importance, especially if you are shopping at brick and mortar stores. It is in your best interest to get to know your local area and follow our guidelines for the best times to shop. Additionally, you need to choose which path you will take when plotting the course: Will you choose to specialize, go general, or pursue a combination of the two? Regardless of the path you take, if you are armed with a realistic budget, know your product, understand market conditions, and connect with the sellers, you have developed a recipe for your long-term success.

Chapter 6
THE ONLINE SUCCESS BLUEPRINT:
Becoming a Resale Millionaire

uilding a business reliant on finding treasures in other people's trash takes time, patience, and know-how. For us, the motivation began as a way to spend quality time with one another. But as we collected more and more items, we simply had to make more room in our treasure-filled house. So we quickly determined the next logical step was to take some of the most exciting and unique items and see if we could sell them for a small profit. But the excitement of taking these gems and then selling them online for profit was amazingly satisfying, and was representative of more than just a financial gain. We put our all into it, and learned a lot along the way, and we couldn't have done it without the Internet. This chapter will offer you the blueprint for building a successful online business. There is no time like the present to make a full transition and become a *Resale Millionaire.*

To Infinity and Beyond: The Value of the Internet

There are many important figures through out history that haven't accurately predicted the future, with perhaps Nostradamus being the most famous. Another notable character was Charles H. Duell, the Commissioner of the US patent office in 1899. Mr. Duell's most famous attributed utterance is that "everything that can be invented has been invented." Clearly, Mr. Duell was more than a little off base given the enormous amount of inventions since the beginning of the 1900s. One of the most important inventions of the last 100 years was undoubtedly the computer, and subsequently the Internet. Like Duell, not very many people were able to accurately predict what was coming, as is evidenced below:

"The internet is just a fad" — *Newsweek*, Feb. 26,1995

"Almost all of the many predictions now being made about 1996 hinge on the Internet's continuing exponential growth. But I predict the Internet will soon go spectacularly supernova and in 1996 catastrophically collapse." — *Robert Metcalfe, founder of 3Com, 1995*

"I think there is a world market for maybe five computers." — *Thomas Watson, president of IBM, 1943*

"There is no reason anyone would want a computer in their home." — *Ken Olsen, founder of Digital Equipment Corporation, 1977*

Oops!!! However, to be fair, the reality is that even for the most intelligent and successful among us, it is nearly impossible to predict the future. This is especially true when it comes to the Internet because it is still in the very early stages of its impact on business and on our day-to-day living. With that said, although we may not be able to predict the future, we can understand the general framework of the benefits and pitfalls currently available to us when we embark on our journey as online retailers. Let's take a look at some of the benefits of selling online.

Benefits of Selling Online

- No storefront required—you don't need to rent a physical location, build out the location, or sign a long-term lease.
- You can sell products without having to stock large amounts of inventory to fill your storefront.
- Customers can purchase product directly from your website without the help of expensive sales and customer service staff.
- You can reach a global audience without having to open locations across the globe.
- You can make sales 24 hours a day, seven days a week.
- You have the ability to reach your target clients with the click of the mouse.
- You have the ability to engage in real-time conversations.
- You can work from any location with an Internet connection.

Most businesses can launch e-commerce sites without any significant investment. Companies like 3Dcart, Volusion, Shopify, and others will provide templates for your shop, and they even have free trials and ongoing costs below $50 a month.

Whatever form of online shop you choose, it's important to take a strategic view. Even if you don't plan to do the majority of your business online, it is beneficial for you to have a website. For example, maybe you are in the service business and it is not practical for your clients to make a purchase without you physically inspecting the job. Ask yourself, what benefits could your customers receive from your online presence? If you are a plumber, maybe you could give them information on how to turn off the water to that overflowing toilet that woke them up in the middle of the night, or maybe they could book their service call for the next morning without having to talk to your office. They could also create an account, have access to their service history, make online payments, rate and review their experience, or recommend your service to friends and family.

The simple fact remains that regardless of the type of business you are in, each year more and more of your customers are online and connected to the Internet. If you want to remain relevant, you need to be where your customers are: It really is that simple. We live in a digital age, and staying current is of the utmost importance.

Avoid Online Pitfalls

Regardless of your online goals, there are some common pitfalls to avoid, which will ensure your customers do not become frustrated:

- *Accuracy*—Make sure your website information is updated on a regular basis so that out-of-date or incorrect information is quickly removed.
- *Keep It Simple*—Make sure site navigation and the purchase process are simple and easy.
- *Don't over commit and underperform*—Make sure you can deliver on any promises you make.
- *Lack of customer support*—Just because you are online does not mean your customers no longer want to speak to you. Make sure your customers can engage with you on their terms.
- *Lack of product and business information*—Determine what questions your consumers have, what objections, concerns, fears, etc., and address those concerns on your website. You can include this information on product, about us, and informational pages.
- *Poor visual design*—Nothing will kill your brand image quicker than a cheap and poorly designed website. Make sure your website is professionally designed and easy to use.

- *Remove the Risk*—Failure to remove the risk in the transaction is one of the largest pitfalls we encounter. By giving your customers a 100% money-back guarantee, you remove significant friction from the sales process.
- *Poor Product Images*—Make sure the images on your site are accurate and show products or services in their best possible light.
- *Failure to Communicate*—Make sure you confirm orders immediately by email and notify customers with shipment and tracking information. Your customers want to be kept in the loop, not in the dark.

Creating an online business is exciting and promising, but it does not come without risk. While there are many benefits to operating and owning an online business, there are also many pitfalls. Figure out what purpose your website will serve, and find the time and resources to build it correctly and effectively.

Opportunity Galore: Pick Your Poison

If you search "make money online" on Google, you will get over 500 million-search results. These results will include the general areas of List Building, Search Engine Optimization (SEO), Social Marketing, Traffic Generation, Link Building, Affiliate Marketing, Blogging, E-commerce, eBay, Amazon, Etsy, Video Marketing, Internet Marketing, and the list goes on.

Although there are countless ways to make money online, the two main markets are the selling of information based products and services, and the selling of physical goods and services. As *Resale Millionaires*, we are going to focus on the buying and selling of physical products.

Whether you're just starting your first online venture, or you just want to make some extra money online, we want you to hit the ground running. And because success loves positive action (and so does your wallet), the following 10 tips are designed to give you focus and direct your efforts regardless of your ultimate goals.

10 Great Ways to Find Products to Sell Online

- *Garage, Estate, and Bazaar Sales*—These are your bread and butter events. Don't get discouraged if you shop a few duds out of the gate because finding great deals is often more of a marathon than a sprint. Stay with it and you will be rewarded.
- *Local markets*—If your area has a local merchant market, then go there and look around for anything that fits your objectives. If you shop often enough you may make some friends with the market traders and gain valuable insights on what products are great sellers and what trade shows they attend. And you may even gain a few inside supplier tips!
- *Pawnshops*—Pawnshops tend to accumulate a lot of inventory and like any business, they need to convert that inventory into cash. Generally, pawnshops' bread and butter are jewelry, gold, silver, and coins. In some areas, guns and hunting related equipment are staples as well. Items that fall outside of their core area of expertise usually end up haphazardly placed throughout the store. Search around for items that don't seem to match their core business; chances are these items have been in the shop for a while, so you can get a great deal. Also, if you can find a group of items, you can negotiate a bundle or bulk deal.
- *Real auctions*—Go to your local auction houses because chances are you can resell things for more than what it will cost you to buy them. After all, they only have a few hundred customers in that room on a good night—you have millions to sell to online! Just avoid getting into any emotional bidding wars and you will do fine. Remember to bring your smart phone so that you can

check online prices for items you have an interest in ahead of your bidding.

- *Local ads*—Place an ad in the local papers that reads, "I pay cash for [whatever items you want to buy]." We suggest you set up an email account that you only use for this purpose, and avoid giving out your phone number.
- *Ad boards*—Many of your local coffee shops, restaurants, and grocery stores have ad boards for their customers to utilize; these can work for both buying and selling of your merchandise.
- *Friends*—Let friends and family know what you are doing. Ask them to keep their eyes open for any promising looking sales. See if they have anything they'd like to get rid of and ask them to spread the word to their friends.
- *Get The Word Out* —Give out business cards, and tell people what you do. Chances are you'll come across someone who'll say, "Oh, really? I've got a load of [items] I don't want."
- *Discount Retailers*—This might be a little surprising, but there are many opportunities to purchase at these retailers and make nice profits selling online. Take a look around your local deep discounter, and pay special attention to any national brand names.
- *Online Marketplaces*—Most people don't realize that eBay, Amazon, and Woot are actually terrific places to find products and product-sourcing ideas. Type the word bulk in your search query and you will often find larger lots that you can buy and then resell in smaller quantities for a nice profit.

We Have All This Great Stuff, NOW WHAT?

We have gone through the process of identifying sales, picking niches, doing our homework, and getting the best deals—now the real fun begins. It is time to convert our acquired treasures into cash, and the two best places to do this are Amazon.com and eBay.com. Let's learn a bit about these companies since we will be spending a lot of time working with them.

History of eBay.com

eBay is an online auction website that was founded as AuctionWeb in San Jose, California, on September 5, 1995 by Iranian-American computer programmer Pierre Omidyar. One of the first items sold on eBay was a broken laser pointer for $14.83. Astonished, Omidyar contacted the winning bidder to ask if he understood that the laser pointer was broken. In his responding email, the buyer explained: "I'm a collector of broken laser pointers." A new market was born.

The frequently repeated story that eBay was founded to help Omidyar's fiancée trade Pez candy dispensers was fabricated by a public relations manager in 1997 because the media was not interested in the company's previous explanation about wanting to create a "perfect market." This marketing scheme was revealed in Adam Cohen's 2002 book, *The Perfect Store*, and was later confirmed by eBay. The company officially changed the name of its service from AuctionWeb to eBay in September of 1997.

In 1997, the company received $6.7 million in funding from the venture capital firm Benchmark Capital. Meg Whitman was hired as eBay President and CEO in March of 1998. At the time, the company had 30 employees, half a million users, and revenues of $4.7 million in the United States. eBay went public on September 21, 1998. eBay's target share price of $18 was all but ignored as the price went to $53.50 on the first day of trading.

Millions of collectibles, decor, appliances, computers, furnishings, equipment, domain names, vehicles, and other miscellaneous items are listed, bought, and sold daily on eBay. In 2006, eBay launched its Business & Industrial category, breaking into the industrial surplus business. Generally, anything can be auctioned on the site as long as it is not illegal and does not violate the eBay Prohibited and Restricted Items policy. Services and intangibles can be sold too.

History of Amazon.com

Amazon is an American multinational electronic commerce company with headquarters in Seattle, Washington. It is the world's largest online retailer. The company also produces consumer electronics—most notably the Amazon Kindle e-book reader and the Kindle Fire tablet computer—and it is a major provider of cloud computing services.

Jeff Bezos incorporated the company as Cadabra in July 1994, and the site went online as Amazon.com in 1995.[34] The company was renamed after the Amazon River, one of the largest rivers in the world, as well as after the Amazons, the legendary nation of female warriors in Greek mythology. Amazon.com started as an online bookstore, but soon diversified selling DVDs, CDs, MP3 downloads, software, video games, electronics, apparel, furniture, food, toys, and jewelry.

Amazon was spurred by what Bezos called his "regret minimization framework," which he described as his effort to fend off regret for not staking a claim in the Internet gold rush.

Amazon's initial business plan was unusual, as the company did not expect a profit for four to five years. Its "slow" growth provoked stockholder complaints that the company was not reaching profitability fast enough. When the dot-com bubble burst, and many e-companies went out of business, Amazon persevered, and finally turned its first profit in the fourth quarter of 2001: $5 million or 1¢ per share, on revenues of more than $1 billion. The profit, although it was modest, served to demonstrate that the business model could be profitable.

Feel free to do some more research on eBay and Amazon because chances are you will sell lots of product on these sites.

Payment Methods

Each marketplace has their own policy on accepted payment methods. While there are restricted payment methods, most marketplaces provide choices to sellers and buyers that are convenient and accessible. We have found the utilizing of PayPal to be a very simple and cost effective way to send and receive payments across multiple platforms.

Most clients also prefer to use PayPal, which is a guaranteed sure and safe way to pay for the items you have purchased online. With PayPal, you simply need a credit card or bank account and email address. PayPal can also be used to pay for your shipping through both Amazon and eBay.

Setting up a PayPal Account

Here are the steps for how to start up your PayPal account and use it for your purchases:

- **Step 1:** Go to the PayPal site and choose the type of account that you need. You can choose whether you need a personal, premier, or business account.
- **Step 2:** Provide your personal information, such as your name, address, email address, and use these to register for an account. You will need to use your email address to login to your account.
- **Step 3:** You also need to verify your identity by providing your bank account information. You can give your credit card number or your debit card details. The verification process will involve a small transaction so that they can verify your account.
- **Step 4:** You can also choose to link your bank accounts to PayPal so that you can easily transfer money when using PayPal. We highly recommend you do this because you can avoid higher fees associated with credit cards or your bank account should

you need to spend more than the cash balance in your account at any given time.

Creating an eBay Account

Setting up an eBay account is just as easy as signing up for PayPal. Just follow these simple steps:

Step 1: Set up your seller account by confirming the personal information that you have submitted to eBay. You need to verify your identity and choose an automatic payment method for the fees you need to pay as a seller, and for reimbursements. You can read through the eBay Buyer Protection Policy to understand more about the claims. Having your PayPal account verified will also be helpful as eBay will need to confirm your identity and credibility as a seller.

Step 2: You can now create your listing! eBay will guide you to ensure that you can make a list of the items that you wish to sell. You provide a description of the items and eBay can help you categorize them properly. eBay also helps you determine a suggested market price for your item.

Step 3: Start selling now! You can already sell the items on your list! Make sure that you read the rules for sellers and familiarize yourself with the eBay policies and restrictions so you know what to do and what not to do when completing a transaction.

Combining PayPal and eBay

You can also directly set up a PayPal account on your eBay account by following these steps:

- **Step 1:** Go to your eBay account and navigate to the "My eBay" page so you can see your eBay account summary.

- **Step 2:** Go to the "Account" tab so you can start setting up your PayPal account.
- **Step 3:** Click "PayPal Account" to begin the registration process. If you already have a current PayPal account, you can just choose to link it with your eBay account. You can also create a new account from this tab. You will be directed to the PayPal site, and after providing all the necessary information you can click the "Return to eBay" button.
- **Step 4:** In order for you to complete the linking process, you simply have to click "Link my PayPal Account."

Choosing your Username

Branding is extremely important in your online business; therefore, you want to ensure you are as consistent as possible across the entire web.

Choose a username that matches your web URL. If you want your eBay username to be "TheBestDealsEver," make sure you can also get the domain name: www.TheBestDealsEver.com. Choosing your username is an important decision, but do not worry if you miss out on the ideal username initially, as eBay does allow you to change your username once every 30 days. eBay will place an icon next to your username indicating you changed your name and they will transfer over all your ratings and listings. Another thing to consider when picking a username is that you want your name to reflect what you will be selling.

You also want to provide yourself some flexibility as you grow your business, or as the market changes. Eddies8Tracks was a great username until cassettes, CDs, MP3s, and satellite radio took over. Instead, usernames like EddiesMusic or EddiesTunes are specific enough to inform your customers of what you sell, and they are still brandable without boxing you in as things change. If you are not sure what you will sell long term, choose a name like KimsDeals, SallieSeashells, or KarensBargains.

Spend some time brainstorming your username before you log onto eBay to open your account. Avoid using numbers in your username unless the number is extremely relevant to your offering like Route66Signs; on the other hand, using Karen3 is not memorable and can be confusing for your buyers. You can also pick a fun or whimsical username as long as it is easy to remember.

Niche Online Marketplaces

Although eBay and Amazon are the two largest marketplaces for selling your items online, they are by no means the only online marketplaces. There are thousands of niche marketplaces where you can buy, sell and trade. A couple of standouts are Gazelle and Etsy.

Gazelle is an online market place where you can buy and sell consumer electronics like computers and smartphones. One of the unique features of Gazelle is that they publish their purchase prices for various electronic devices. Knowing you can sell an item for a specified price allows you to take all the guess work out of selling, and allows you to know your profit immediately based on your purchase price and Gazelle's published buy price.

The Gazelle story began in 2007 with a simple question: If you can trade in a used car, why can't you trade in a used phone or other electronic device? The answer: a new business was born.

Gazelle.com was launched in 2008, and offered a simple online trade-in service with instant quotes and free shipping. In 2014, Gazelle launched a store to sell certified pre-owned devices.

Gazelle is the nation's leading consumer electronics trade-in site; they have handled more than 2 million consumer devices and paid out more than $200 million for all kinds of electronic devices.

Another great niche online market is Etsy, which was founded in June 2005 by Rob Kalin in his Brooklyn apartment. The goal of Etsy was to fill a need for an online community where crafters, artists, and makers could sell their handmade and vintage goods and craft supplies.

Today, Etsy is a global community connecting some 20 million users and 1.5 million sellers around the globe, and they have amassed nearly $2 billion a year in merchandise sales. Their community features products you can't find anywhere else.

Maximizing the Deal: Lining Your Pockets

In December of 2013, the Brain Research Center reported that the average return of items purchased at garage sales and sold on eBay was an amazing 462%. The bad news was that the average purchase price of garage sale items was only .85 cents, resulting in a meager $3.93 return. Dealing with the average garage sale items at a $3.93 profit would keep you busy, broke, and frustrated. So if you are thinking there must be a better way, you are correct—it's called the "Bread and Butter" strategy.

With the "Bread and Butter" strategy you want to focus on items you can purchase for less than about $15 and sell for around $60. It has been our experience that items priced and acquired in these general price ranges result in low holding costs, greater returns on your time, and they are priced attractively for the majority of online shoppers. The items that typically fall into the "Bread and Butter" category include jewelry, watches, figurines, art, handbags, wallets, fashion items, collectibles, vintage Americana, signs, posters, household items, sports equipment, and camping gear.

Does this mean we only sell items around $60? Absolutely not, if we can buy items for a buck and sell them for $10, $15, $20, we sometimes will—these low cost items are referred to as smalls. They are not items you should build your business around, unless you have a unique niche market. We also purchase items we plan to sell for hundreds or even thousands of dollars—these items are referred to as profit maximizes.

Again, these are not our core "Bread and Butter" items, but when the opportunity presents itself, we will take advantage of it.

Negotiating the Best Prices

You know what you want to buy and sell, and where you can buy and sell, but now we want to make sure know how to get the best deals. The following sections will teach you how to negotiate like a seasoned pro.

Building Rapport

Rapport is defined as a relation characterized by harmony, conformity, accord, or affinity. There are many books written on this topic and they discuss everything from mirroring body language and speech to facial language and dress. The critical fact to remember is this—we all like people who we perceive to be like us.

When I pull up to a garage sale, I immediately pay attention to every detail: Is the yard well manicured and cared for? Is there a particular bumper sticker on the car in the driveway? Is there anything special about the car I can bring up? Is there team memorabilia from a local sports team for sale? Are there any unique photos or posters from a location I have visited? Do they collect Disney, Barbie, or trains?

The purpose of all this is to establish a quick connection with the seller. Building rapport starts with a great smile and a pleasant hello. The next step is to get them to tell you about themselves, or about an item for sale, their pet, kid, really just about anything will do. You just want to create a conversation and find something you have in common. The goal is to connect on a personal level and separate yourself from the other people who are in a hurry to get to the next sale.

Getting the seller talking will not only help you make a connection, it will also give you valuable insights into why they are conducting a sale. This opens the door for additional follow up questions, which help you prepare your buying strategy. Building rapport is a simple and effective way to get the best possible deals. Remember, most of us love to hear the sound of our own voice and are happy to tell you more than you really want to hear!

Estate sale strategy is the nearly same, but you have to remember the person charged with selling the items in the estate sale has no personal connection with any of the items. When visiting estate sales, I like to comment on how well organized the sale is, how I love the amount of work they did staging items, and what a wonderful marketing job they did promoting the sale.

If I cannot honestly comment on the quality of the sale, I will simply ask questions like, "How has the sale been going? Anything special you think I should look at? How long have you been in the business?" You get the general idea. One thing to remember is that a lot of work has gone into preparing for the sale, and the estate sale company's staff is often tired from all the prep work. When approaching the staff, you want to be respectful and ensure they are not processing a sale or helping another customer.

By building relationships, you may be first to learn about upcoming sales, unsold items, or insider tips on items you specialize in. Estate sale companies depend on regulars to help them sell their items. Although some companies may utilize online auctions in their business, most estate sale companies rely on local marketing and need to sellout at the sale. Since you have more flexibility, time, and access to millions of customers online, you can create significant profit opportunities.

Doing Your Homework

Information and knowledge are the foundation for your negotiating success. For example, you must know what you can sell an item for, how long it is likely to take to sell, and what will it cost to ship. Armed with this knowledge, you can avoid getting caught up in the emotion of the moment and ultimately avoid making a bad purchase decision.

Breaking the Ice

Breaking the ice simply means completing your first transaction with the seller. If you are interested in purchasing some expensive items, one great strategy is to find a lower priced item and just purchase it at the seller's asking price. For this transaction, you are not worried about the best price, you just want to get the money flowing and build a relationship. Once you have built rapport and broken the ice, you are in position to start making the best deals you can on the larger, more expensive items.

Bundling

One of our favorite strategies is called bundling. With this strategy, you combine items to create a higher dollar transaction in total, but a lower per item cost for you. This works with everything from the box of sports cards to kitchen appliances and even with totally unrelated items. We once got a box of 300 vintage music pins for $20 when they were asking $1 for each pin. Another time we were able to negotiate three vintage jewelry boxes and a penholder for $100, and later sold each individual item for well over $100 each.

We have bundled books, sports cards, clothing, comics, records, baskets, plants, posters, household items, ties, and jewelry for fractions of their individual unit prices. On some occasions we have even bought everything in an entire room! Bundling is a great strategy you can use with just two items, or an entire household. Remember, the seller wants these items gone!

Cash in Hand

There is something about staring at the cash in your hand that legitimizes your offer in the seller's mind. You are offering them cash money *right now*. You are not asking them to hold the item, you are not offering them a check—you have cold hard cash, and that resonates with the seller at a different level. Having cash allows you to tap into the impulsive emotional aspect of the seller's personality. Cash is King!

Condition Issues

Small issues with condition—a missing piece, no box or damaged boxed, a crack, a tear, a fold, a missing book jacket, or basically any condition issue—can and should be used to reduce the price of the item and make it appear less valuable to the seller. Just take care not to be a jerk or be disrespectful. You can often simply ask a question like, "Is that a crack in the side of this pottery piece? Do you have the box to go with it? Did you notice the blemish right here?" You would be surprised at how many times we hear, "I did not notice that," followed by the seller offering the item at a steep discount. It is worth asking!

Situational Awareness

According to *Webster's Dictionary*, situational awareness is the perception of environmental elements with respect to time and/or space, the comprehension of their meaning, and the projection of their status after some variable has changed, such as time, or some other variable, such as a predetermined event. Wow, that is a mouthful! Let's simplify this definition for you:

What we are talking about when we refer to situational awareness is a simple understanding of the constraints facing the seller. Did they sell the house and have to be out at the end of the week? Are they moving in three days and all items most go? Are they downsizing and have no place for that large piano? Is this the last hour of the Estate Sale? Are the sellers facing foreclosure?

Understanding the seller's motivations and constraints allows you to negotiate the best deal. We are not looking to take advantage of individuals, we are looking to understand their situation and frame our offer in a fashion that will help them achieve their desired overall outcome.

When it comes to negotiating, there are many different techniques and tactics. Ultimately, you have to find what works for you, but to get you started we have compiled what works for us:

Five Best Negotiating Practices

1. Great negotiators are great listeners. By listening, observing behavior, and being attentive, you can learn things that will help you get the best deal. You'll learn more by asking open-minded questions than you will by simply talking.

2. To paraphrase an old cliché, the three most important things about a negotiation are preparation, preparation, and preparation. Know what your item can be sold for online, determine your minimum acceptable profit margin, and set your highest purchase price.

3. Don't be afraid to ask. Becoming a good negotiator starts with overcoming one's own fears. Do not worry about insulting the sellers; you will likely never see them again. To paraphrase another old cliché, practice makes perfect. Get out and start negotiating!

4. Never negotiate against yourself. Once you make your offer, wait for a response from the seller. By waiting, you avoid the possibility of stepping on your own offer and making further concessions before a seller has stated their position.

5. It's okay to make the first offer! Contrary to popular belief, the first person to throw out a number doesn't always lose. If you have done your homework, built rapport, and have good situational awareness, it is perfectly acceptable to start the negotiations.

This chapter has provided you with an online success blueprint that brings you one step closer to becoming a *Resale Millionaire.* You are now knowledgeable about the value of doing business on the Internet, and are savvy about different online marketplaces. You learned how pick an effective username and set up online marketplace accounts. You know how to avoid common pitfalls, and you know where to shop to find the best products to sell online. In addition, you have learned proven buying techniques and negotiating practices. Now you are ready to start your online business—so get to work and start making money!

Chapter 7

THE MARKETING PLAN:
Connecting with your Customers

*N*ow that we have detailed the global view to create an online blueprint, let's shift our focus to building a thoughtful marketing plan and connecting with our consumers. As with every business, marketing and promotion are essential elements to success. If the customers cannot see you, you'll never have a chance to create a prosperous business. Becoming a *Resale Millionaire* starts with acquiring the goods and building an online success blueprint, but the real difference-maker is the manner in which you market and promote your business through an online presence. We can call it your online fingerprint, unique to your own business, and leaving a lasting impression everywhere you have been. Separating yourself from the competition and creating a detailed and rigorous marketing plan is essential to the growth and management of your business. This chapter will give you vital tools to implement this plan and launch your business in the direction of the moon and the stars.

The Gold Standard: Creating a Marketable Website

Launching your business used to mean selecting a physical storefront location to get things started. The biggest decision may have once been picking the signage on the front of your business. But boy have times changed. As an online business owner, your business interacts with customers online, where they play by their own rules. They can have direct contact with your business from the comforts of their own home, with little direct impact from you or your staff. That which you created before they arrived is all they will know. So the key decision that now remains is the manner in which you build your online presence. From our perspective, your online presence should accomplish four essential goals:

1. Engage your customer
2. Share your mission/purpose
3. Inform your consumer of who/what you are
4. Convert visitors into paying customers

The best way to accomplish these goals is to create your own website. Your website becomes a "base camp" for all your online efforts. You own this "base camp," and you control want happens there through establishing the rules. This is a critical point, as social media sites that are popular today are often yesterday's news in just a few short years. But your website will always remain in the limelight. While most popular social media sites start out free, their growth usually comes with a desire to monetize their business. So what was once given is now paid for; but you can ensure you can continue to interact with your customers on your terms by creating your own website.

As an example, Facebook recently changed the rules on how many people actually see your posts. Let's say you spent tens of thousands of dollars building your Facebook page and one day you awake to find the rules changed. Shockingly, now only about 15% of your audience will even see one of your posts. Now you have to pay to promote your posts if you want to reach all those folks you worked so hard to curate! Great for the folks at Facebook, but not so great for your business. We are not picking on Facebook here, because every social media site goes through changes like these. But we do want to highlight why it is important for you to own your own site and control your own conversations. Just like your business, these sites want to build profits. They play the same game you do. So unless you have an endless marketing budget, the trick is picking your battles. Social media is a great tool, but it is only one piece of the overall pie; one over which you have little control. Sadly, you play by their rules, not yours. Since the rules do and will continue change, it is important you create a "base camp" or a place of comfort that you can always call your own.

So with that said, what is the key to developing a great website? Great websites make it easy for their users to connect with the information in which they contact. You will find success if your design is easy to navigate and captures the interest of the user. You want to think through the objectives of the audience you are targeting and then make it easy for them to achieve their goals.

Uploading your business to the Internet is one of the most effective things you can do to directly reach and interact with customers. It is all about access. But it does not have to be costly. Remember, content is king. Utilizing freelance sites like Elance.com can curb the cost, offering an opportunity to build a site by a freelancer for under $500. Additionally, simple tools like WordPress allow freelancers to quickly and cost effectively customize a site for your specific needs.

When utilizing web strategies to grow your businesses, take the time to pay close attention to how your customers are engaging with your site. Utilizing tools like Google Analytics will help you improve your site flow and user conversions by providing you with features such as data collection and management, data consolidation, analysis reports, and data activation. Using Google Analytics will allow you to make informed marketing decisions for your site by providing you the information you need to target and win the consumers you desire. The best way to get a return on your online investment is to make sure it's telling your story easily, succinctly, and accurately.

With that said, here are a few of our favorite tips to ensure you are headed in the right direction:

1. Have a clear message

Your goal is to immediately provide clarity surrounding your business. Studies show you have less than three seconds to grab your reader's attention.[35] Thus, you need to take the time to make your services or products crystal clear. Since websites lead with imaging, pay close attention to your images and what they represent. Think about what your website does. Think about what you want it to do. What products or services do you offer? Based on your response, clearly display that message in the content on your homepage. Many websites fail to communicate the essence of their brands to customers, and thereby lose leads and sales. Your website is often a potential customer's first impression of your business, so make it count.

2. Simplify it

Organize the content on your website in a simple and structured way. Think of the general path you would like a site visitor to take. Often, adding category tabs to the top or side bar navigation will be the best option for organizing your information into specific buckets, enabling consumers to easily navigate your site. Tabs or categories like "reviews," "similar items," and "products" will allow your users to have a better experience, which will support your growth and additional sales.

3. Content is King

The main function of your website is to create sales. In order to achieve those coveted sales, you'll want to convey relevant content to your visitors in order to help them understand the problems that your products and/or services may solve for them. Work to ensure the content you add to your site is easy to understand and the language you use is consistent with the language of your target market. You'll want to try to include keywords that are relevant to your business and industry in your content, page titles, meta-tags (snippets of text that describe page content), headings, and product descriptions. Keywords are the words users would type into a search engine to find your business and its products and services.

Content is not just your words, but also your images. Images are typically the first thing people notice about your page. They should grab your customer's attention and provoke emotional connections, as people will be more likely to support your business when they feel directly connected to you.

4. Don't forget to build community

Building a community for your business is one of the keys to leveraging your online presence. We recommend that you start with Pinterest, Facebook and Twitter, as these are three of the most popular and effective social media sites available for business and marketing. Include a Facebook "Like" option for your business Facebook page, a Twitter follow button, and a Pinterest Pin button on your site and within your content. This will allow your visitors to connect and share your products and services via social media. The more clicks, the more presence you'll have. You also may want to consider LinkedIn and Instagram for your business, as they are gaining in popularity as a marketing tool for businesses and consumers. It is better to be effective in a few valued spots rather than trying to be present everywhere. Although signing up for social media accounts typically will not cost you any initial investment, social media isn't really "free." To effectively engage in social media, you'll want to take the time to understand how each opportunity actually works and exactly how you can maximize your exposure and minimize your cost/risk. Regardless, we have found it is definitely worth the financial investment.

5. Integrate a blog as part of your website

Remember that people do business with those they trust and deem as experts. So, the manner in which you disseminate information and teach your consumer will often create leverage for you and your business. Creating and maintaining a blog as part of your website is one of the most effective ways to engage and build community. Blogs allow you to demonstrate your expertise, engage in a wide range of topics, and since they create fresh content, they are great for driving keyword search rankings. Through utilizing keyword tools, you can see exactly which terms users are inputting to find the products and services you offer. Armed with this knowledge, you can then write blog posts to specifically target these users and grow your sales. Content rich websites are valued at a higher level by Google and other search engine sites. So, the more content you create and post to your site, the greater likelihood you'll see organic growth within the search engine results.

6. Make it easy for people to reach you

This may seems like a basic point, but it's critical that your contact information on your site is easy to find and up-to-date. By making it easy for customers to reach you, you will build credibility and trust. If people have a hard time connecting with you, they'll doubt your commitment to customer services and support. Make sure your phone number, address and email are prominently displayed and easy to find. Additionally, offer consumers the opportunity to reach out to you through a "one-click" option. Offering numerous ways in which to reach you will build trust and allow consumers an opportunity to choose exactly how they want to do business with you. Often times, it is customer service and accessibility that wins consumers over.

7. Build your search engine rankings

How does your site appear in search engine results? How are people searching for your type of business? Natural search rankings can really drive traffic to your website. About 75% of people never go past the first page of search results. Investing in SEO services can help you develop a plan for content on your site that will help improve your rankings. But we are of the school of thought that content rich websites will always be the ones that offer a greater opportunity to be seen.

8. Video

Videos from YouTube show up directly in search engine results. Thus, adding video to your content can jump-start your search engine ranking. In fact, this is quickly becoming one of the strongest ways to increase visibility. Pay close attention to your video titles for SEO and make sure you utilize key search terms in your title. Video is frequently shared and also will help you reach a bigger audience, as Google and other search engines give video content extremely high value.

9. Build a brand

Make sure your website looks and feels consistent with the look of your business cards, brochures and other promotional materials. Inconsistency can confuse your customers and result in lost sales. Consistency across your entire customer interactions will demonstrate your professionalism and help build trust with potential customers. Thus, you should create and then maintain one logo that you use on your site, your business cards, your resume, your invoices, your packaging slips, and your letterhead. That small but important step creates trust and a showing of expertise.

10. Build a List

Ask site visitors for their email address via an "opt in" box or exit pop up form. To encourage visitors to give you their email address, offer something for free, give a special discount, provide a special report, newsletter, eBook, inside tips, or something else of value. Services like AWeber or MailChimp make it simple and easy to integrate forms and opt in boxes on your website and successfully build your email list via your website. Once you build a list, provide your consumers with content rich offerings and keep them posted with exciting industry updates. By doing this, you build relationships with your consumer and keep them at the top of your mind.

At the end of the day, there are enormous opportunities available for you to create visibility, grow presence, and maintain consumer contact. By taking all or most of these steps, you'll begin to nurture your business and watch it grow.

The Social Media Scramble

Facebook, Twitter, Instagram, oh my! There is an enormous array of social media opportunities on which you can hang your hat. For every big success story we hear about while marketing on Facebook, we also hear 10 other stories of, "Oh, I tried that, but it didn't go anywhere so I gave up." So does marketing on Facebook work? Without question it does. Facebook is the most visited website in the world, and getting fans can mean a significant boost for your business. But the key is to have a game plan for how you're going to build, brand, and market yourself on social media. With that in mind, we've put together this list of tips to get you moving in the right direction.

Building your business with Facebook

First, create a Facebook page. Sounds simple, right? It is, but the problem is marketers get confused and they start a profile instead of a page. Profiles are meant for non-commercial use (individuals), while pages are commercial (businesses, brands, organizations). If you want to market your business on Facebook, a profile simply won't cut it. Pages are meant for businesses and they are much more effective at getting your message out there. Once you decide to actually build a business page, you next have to begin the growth of it. The following are some of the best tips we can offer to optimize your Facebook business page:

- *Promote your fan page.* First, place your fan page URL in your email signature. Now, every time you send an email, it's another chance for recipients to find your Facebook fan page.
- *Cross page promote your page.* By posting on other fan pages using your page's username, you'll find a visible link to your page with each comment.
- *Consider purchasing Facebook ads.* It's easy: you can spend as little as you like, and you can target your campaigns to only those people who are likely to be interested in what you have to offer.
- *Convert consumers into fans.* We've touched on this, but it's important: Give people a great reason to become your fan. Maybe it's to get discounts or updates. Maybe it's a free video, eBook, etc. Just make sure it's something that motivates immediate and swift action.
- *Add your page URL to YouTube.* Do you create videos to promote your business? Then by all means add your fan-page URL link to your videos, either at the end of the video or at the beginning of the video description to create visibility.

- *Post frequently.* If you forget about your fan-page, your fans will forget about you. Post once or twice a day with meaningful info, updates, and questions. Don't make it all about you and your products. Instead, post about events, news, your industry, and so forth. And whenever you can, inject a little humor into the mix.

- *Utilize your fans.* Ask your fans to like your content so it gets shared on their walls. You can't ask every time, but it is perfectly appropriate to do so every now and again. When they like your post, more people will see it, which can lead to more fans and greater visibility. Get your fans involved with your page by starting discussions about your products and services or industry news. What's the best way to start a discussion? Simply ask a provocative question your fans cannot ignore. If you get stuck on what to ask, use the fill in the blank kind of question, such as, "If you could live anywhere in the world, it would be _____."

- *Do not become a troll victim.* Now that you're starting discussions, remember to remain professional at ALL TIMES, with no exceptions. If you are perceived as quarreling with a fan, it won't matter if you're right—it will only matter that you lost your cool and you look like a real idiot. Always remain a true professional.

- *Use photos and videos.* Written words are great, but videos are better and photos tend to get shared. So incorporate a variety of mediums into your Facebook communications.

- *Brand your page.* That large image on your timeline needs to stand out. It should effectively communicate the message you want to send to your fans, so spend some time getting it just right.

- *Keep track.* Use Facebook insights to discover when people are most engaged with your content. This way you know when to post to get the maximum effect.
- *Encourage return visits.* Facebook check-in deals allow you to offer special incentives when people check in with your page.
- *Use sponsored stories.* Let's say one of your fans writes a great post about you or your business. You can pay to highlight this so there's a better chance it'll be seen.
- *Keep it short and sweet.* Want to capture the most eyeballs? Then keep your posts to 140 characters or less. Longer posts tend to be skimmed over, and shorter ones tend to get read.

Facebook truly offers an amazing opportunity to directly reach consumers in a highly focused manner. As you can see above, there are endless options to optimize content and present it in a meaningful way to your target audience.

Building your business with Pinterest

Pinterest, a visual bookmarking tool, might look like a great way to waste time, but if you dig deeper you realize it's practically made for business. It's likely the only social network where people are actually expecting and looking for images of different products. This means people are often already in a buying mood when they go to Pinterest, and even if they're not, they could be persuaded by the right image. Did you know that pins with price tags included tend to get 36% more likes than pins that don't include price tags?[36] That says a lot about the frame of mind of the typical Pinterest user. If you're interested in having your own Pinterest store to sell your own products, you can set up shop in just minutes with Shop Pinterest. Take advantage of their free trial to see if it's right for you. Here are our favorite tips for using Pinterest to drive traffic to your website:

- *Set up a Pinterest business account.* It's not required, but if you're going to promote via Pinterest, you'll look more professional and credible with a business account.
- *Pick up the "Pin It Button" for your own website.* This lets your readers pin anything they like from your site. (HINT: Do not place photos on your website that you don't want on Pinterest.)
- *Get the board widgets.* This lets visitors follow your boards right from your website.
- *Create internal momentum.* Create at least one board and pin at least several things to it before you begin to build your Pinterest following. Just as you would want to have several posts on a new blog before you begin promoting that blog, you will also want some content before you begin promoting your Pinterest board(s).
- *Understand the options.* Know that a person could follow you, or they could follow a particular board of yours. If they follow you, they will be notified every time you pin to any board. If they follow a single board, they will only be notified when you pin to that board.
- *Use keywords for your boards.* Make each board specific to one set of keywords. By keeping each board tightly focused on one topic, you increase the chances of getting followers who are passionate about that topic.
- *Engage with others.* Pinterest is a social network, so start following other users you think might want to follow you back (think Twitter). Like and comment on their pins.
- *Cross-pollinate.* Promote your Pinterest presence through other channels to get a jump-start on building a following. Notify

your list, your blog readers, your Facebook fans, your Twitter followers, etc.

- *Focus on images.* Use an image for every blog post you make, then pin the image to Pinterest. It should be a strong, attention grabbing image that people would want to share, images are engaging—they hold people to a page longer and get them to read more.
- *Pin photos of happy customers.* If you can, use photos of them either holding your product, using your product, or enjoying the benefits of your product.
- *Add links back to your website in the pin descriptions.* Use a relevant link. For example, link back to the blog post where the image is located. Remember to have an opt-in form on every page of your website so you can capture some of this traffic. And track the leads you get from Pinterest so you can compare your stats with your other marketing venues.
- *Run contests.* Running a "Pin to Win" contest can be a great way to get some Pinterest love quickly. Just make sure you follow the rules because Pinterest has recently tightened its control on contests.
- *Create a user-generated pinboard.* When you let other users (Your top customers? Your most loyal fans?) contribute their own pins to your pinboard, you're involving others in your marketing. Be specific when asking them to contribute. For example, ask them to pin a photo of themselves with your product.
- *Create a video gallery.* Did you know you could also pin videos? Create a board of your best business videos. Mix in some great images too, for peak interest.
- *Use hashtags.* Yes, just like Twitter, Pinterest supports hashtags. You can tag your pins to make them easier to find. Are you rolling out a new product or starting a new campaign? Use the

same hashtag on Pinterest, Twitter, and Google+ to leverage your social media campaign.

We live in a world driven by images. With shrinking attention spans, consumers eat with their eyes first, and if you can monetize pictures, you'll find yourself ahead of the game. So create content rich boards with many pictures highlighting your most successful products.

Building your business with Twitter

Twitter is all about relationships and growing your circle of influence. The better (re: closer) your relationships on Twitter, the more likely people are to re-tweet your stuff, visit your Facebook page and websites, join your lists, and buy your products. So how do you rapidly grow your Twitter following while wielding influence over your followers?

Here are the six best tips we can offer....

- *Be Yourself.* Don't attempt to be Mr. Know-it-All or Ms. Perfect because nobody is buying that nonsense, and even if they were, they want to know they are dealing with real people with real lives, real challenges, and real things to say. Always stay true to yourself because you are a one-of-a-kind original, and as they say, "everyone else is already taken anyway."
- *Appreciate Your Followers.* Re-tweet their best tweets (or the tweets that are the most important to them.) Give them a #FF, which means you're recommending others follow them. Or even send them a direct message. In other words, don't just interact—promote others and expect nothing in return. The more value you can give to others, the more they will like you, appreciate you, and want to reciprocate.
- *Connect With The Big Dogs.* Whatever your niche is, find the influential people in your niche and then engage them. Being

seen with people in authority is one of the quickest ways to be seen as an authority yourself. Plus, their audience will also notice you, and you'll gain followers who hold an avid interest in your particular niche.

- *Engage, Engage, Engage.* Answer the questions of everyone who engages with you, and see how many followers you can engage yourself. You never know who is going to become your next big client or customer—it could be that new guy with only five followers as easily as it could be the seasoned Twitter person with 10,000 followers.

- *Add a Heap of Pizzazz.* We've already said you need to be yourself, and this is perhaps the best advice anyone can give you. But it's okay to take yourself up a notch. You are unique, so go ahead and amplify that uniqueness and be a little larger than life. Be friendlier than you are in real life, be a little bit more flamboyant, go ahead and have opinions and by all means, stand out from the crowd. That last thing you want to do is be a wallflower. And even if you're shy in real life, that's okay. This is the Internet, so it's not like trying to be the life of the party in real life—it's more like portraying yourself in the best light, with the most fun, and the least inhibitions. Frankly, there is no better place for shy people than Twitter; it's a great way to meet tons of people with absolutely zero risk. After all, you don't have to send a tweet until you're certain it says exactly what you want it to say, so you can get it right every time.

- *Have fun.* Need we say more? People like to hang out with people who are having fun, and Twitter is no different. So go ahead, have a blast, let the good times roll, and watch your follower numbers increase accordingly!

If used correctly, Twitter can be a huge asset to your business. Take the time to navigate the waters, and build a community that you can turn into a customer base.

Building your business with YouTube

Most people do not realize that YouTube is the world's second largest search engine.[37] So how can you leverage the power of YouTube? First, tailor your video content to what your viewers want and not necessarily to what you want to show them. In every step, always keep your consumers' preferences in mind during the video making process and put their needs and desires ahead of yours. Next, you've got to vigorously promote your videos. Social sites are often the best way to get the word out. And third, realize that it takes time, resources, and a good idea to make a video people want to watch and pass on to others. And it takes time and resources to properly promote your video. Don't expect to slap up any old video and watch the sales role in. YouTube is a great tool for marketing your business—if you can avoid the following pitfalls:

- Pitfall #1: Thinking all you need to do is upload a video and traffic will flood your website.
  No less than 35 hours of video is uploaded to YouTube every minute, so the competition to get your video seen by viewers is insane. There are tons of high-quality videos that never get more than a few thousand views, and no doubt many more that get even fewer eyeballs.
- *Pitfall #2: Thinking you're too small or new to make video work for you and your business.*
  Just because you need to keep your expectations realistic doesn't mean placing and promoting videos on YouTube won't have an impact on your business. Any business, large or small, can use

video to its advantage. Think about what you like to share with friends and tailor your video accordingly. Even a few thousand views can increase your business, and if you get lucky, you might even create the next video viral sensation.

- *Pitfall #3:* You have to create a commercial video.

  Online video is about engagement with others, not slapping out another "buy my product" commercial. Think of your video as doing much more than simply selling a product or service. People on YouTube want to consume and share engaging and fun content, so don't give them a 20-minute speech on why your product rocks, because odds are they won't watch it. Instead, inject fun, personality and pizzazz into your videos. Make them emotional, or thought provoking, or funny, or all three. Ask yourself: If I saw this video, would I send it to my friends? If the answer is no, then keep working on your concept. Another test to see if you're on the right track: If you were with friends, would you show them the video? If not, then you might want to start over. A video should grab attention and keep the viewer entranced. It should be short—usually less than five minutes and preferably less than a couple minutes. And it should leave the viewer feeling happy they saw it, not happy it's over.

- *Pitfall #4: Trying too hard.*

  You might think you need to spend thousands of dollars to get a professional video created, when the fact is an amateur type of video might do just as well, if not better. People generally don't like "slick" unless it's of a "Hollywood" caliber, and that's expensive. People prefer to watch videos of real people doing real things. To illustrate slick versus real, think of an overly smooth sales person trying to sell you a car—isn't he or she an instant turn off? Now think of an average nice person with a car for sale. She tells you it's a good car, but the heater takes 5 minutes to warm up and it rides a little bumpy. Who do you trust? Or think about the person desperately trying to impress you with how professional he is and how he knows everything about everything, compared again with the average nice person who readily admits she makes bone-headed mistakes and sometimes says or does the wrong thing. Who do you like better?

The bottom line: Do create videos to market your business on YouTube, but don't expect them to get a gazillion views overnight without massive promotion. Be yourself when making the videos, and always keep the viewer in mind through every step of the process.

Creating a Support System

Over the years, we have found that social media can be strongly supported and enhanced by additional steps and specific areas of focus. Extensive blogging, video content, linking social media and websites to one another, and creating a regimented infrastructure to create a brand helps to enhance presence and drive business to you and your company.

These days, if you don't outsource you will find yourself at a significant competitive disadvantage. If you own an internet business, there is just no way around outsourcing and the sooner you embrace this model, the sooner you free yourself of much needed time and effort.

Our go to source for technology, content development, and other tasks is Elance.com, which merged with Odesk.com to form Upwork. com. The Elance platform allows you to post jobs, search for freelance professionals, and solicit proposals. The platform provides ratings and reviews tied to actual jobs performed on the platform and once you select a contractor, communications and files are exchanged through the Elance platform.

Payment for jobs, which can range from hourly-rate to fixed cost per project, is made through Elance's own system. Elance's work management tools provide an official record of communications and work milestones. Funds are held in escrow by Elance to ensure payment is made after work is delivered in accordance with your specified terms.

Fiverr.com is another popular outsource site for small tasks typically costing only $5. We have found that the quality of services varies greatly on Fiverr, but we have had success in the areas of graphic design, banner creation, and social media tasks. When working with Fiverr we typically will hire two or three people for the same task and then select the best submittal for our use. This also protects us should a provider decide to cancel an order right before the due date, or in the case of a provider creating poor quality work. In a nutshell, Fiverr is a great resource, but your experiences will vary greatly, but then again, for $5 you can afford some disappointment from time to time.

If you need more complex or higher quality graphic design work, 99designs.com is the leading outsourcing platform for graphic design including logo design, web design, and other design contents.

Feelancer.com is another popular outsourcing site where you can hire freelancers to do work in areas as diverse as software development, writing, data entry and design, engineering, the sciences, sales and marketing, accounting, and legal services.

The key take away is this: there are companies all over the globe that are designed to help you become more effective and help you achieve your goals. Success in any business depends on how successfully you manage your limited time and resources. Focus your efforts on building a team and leverage the power of outsourcing to get the most out of both your time and money.

For purposes of online marketing, the first conversation should always surround brand analysis and clarity. Once you are hyper-focused on what you represent to the world, you can then shift to building a platform to shine. Creating an informative and brand aware website will start your consumer experience off on the right foot. Once you feel comfortable with your website, start to manifest a relationship between your "base camp" and other landing grounds, like various social media opportunities. The synergy, harmony, and interaction of these are crucial to your overall success. You want to leave a strong online fingerprint, as it is this relationship that will serve you at a high level. Finally, remember to research the avenues out there like Facebook, Pinterest, Twitter, and LinkedIn. There are many more, but these are generally considered to be the Mt. Everest of Social Media. Finally, understand how to evaluate and then optimize these mediums. This can be done through offering consumers rich content, and can be created through a whole number of different ways, many of which are very time and cost sensitive. Don't drop the ball on this.

More than ever, businesses are built through the Internet. If you do not seize this wonderful opportunity, your competitors certainly will. And the best part is that you can do it in your pajamas from the comforts of your own home.

Chapter 8
JOINING THE CLUB:
Opening Up Shop

*M*aria Robinson said, "Nobody can go back and start a new beginning, but anyone can start today and make a new ending." The time is now to start a revolution in your life. This chapter will put the finishing touches on exactly how to identify the right entrepreneurial opportunity for your business, and then how to hit the ground running. Going from part-time to full-time entrepreneur and business owner is not always comforting. It can be scary to consider quitting your day job and taking such a large risk. But the reality is that with our guidance and the information provided in this book, you can successfully create, build, and scale a company with minimal stress and risk. This chapter helps you through rounding out the final touches of fully transitioning into a *Resale Millionaire*, and discusses how we can help you in your journey.

The Passionate Approach to Business

Embrace failure, frustration, and rejection, and keep going. You can't have success without failure, and the sooner you come to grips with this, the more you can succeed. People who enjoy massive success have almost always had massive failure as well.

An integral part of finding out what you're good at and what you can succeed at is discovering what you're not good at. Each failure can move you closer to your goal, if you keep going. A paradigm taught to sales people to help them deal with rejection is to find their closing ratio. For example, if it takes 20 phone calls to get 5 appointments, and 5 appointments to get 2 sales, then that sales person knows that on average they're going to get 15 no's on the phone and another 3 no's in person in order to get 2 sales.

Now instead of dreading no's, the sales person looks forward to them because each no gets them closer to a yes. And so it is with anything you do—you are going to get no's, frustrations, and failures on your way to getting your successes, and that's more than okay, it's great! The person who never fails, also never succeeds.

So resolve to fail your way to the top. The more you try, the more you will fail and the more you will succeed. Turn your frustration into self-motivation and view each failure as both a stepping-stone and a learning tool, and your success will become inevitable.

Our business started as a passion, a love of doing something. Most successful companies are started as a desire to solve a problem or to pursue a passion. Companies that have passionate beginnings are special, as they were born from love, like a newborn baby. Passion is what keeps you going through all the challenges and setbacks; without passion you will likely give up and quit when the going gets tough— and the going will get tough. Passion is the fuel that will allow you to push through the walls, to persist, and ultimately reach the success you desire.

But what if you have a great idea in an area that you're not passionate about? Use the passion behind your idea and apply it to a business or industry that you truly care about. Look at your idea from different vantage points, and you might be surprised by how you can transform your idea into a passion.

Why do you suppose Steve Jobs took a salary of $1 a year? It wasn't just that he wasn't concerned about money—we think he was truly passionate about his company, his products, and changing people's lives. When you love what you're doing, it takes on a life of its own. It's no longer work, it's the highest form of play, and it's also when you're the most successful. One of our favorite quotes is from Steve Jobs' commencement speech, delivered in June 2005:

"Your work is going to fill a large part of your life, and the only way to be truly satisfied is to do what you believe is great work. And the only way to do great work is to love what you do. If you haven't found it yet, keep looking. Don't settle. As with all matters of the heart, you'll know when you find it. And, like any great relationship, it just gets better and better as the years roll on. So keep looking until you find it. Don't settle."

If you look into the history of most success stories, most all of them are rooted in failure. Their passion provides a perfect example of why failure should never stop you from following your dreams.

Most people have heard of Milton Hershey of Hershey candy bar fame, but when Milton Hershey first started his candy empire, he was an unknown. After being fired from an apprenticeship with a printer, Hershey started three separate candy-related ventures, and all of them failed.

In one last attempt, Hershey founded the Lancaster Caramel Company, and started seeing some positive results. Believing in his vision and passion for milk chocolate, he went on to found the Hershey Company, and created one of the most well-known brands in the world.

Before George Steinbrenner became the talk of late night talk show hosts and the owner of the New York Yankees, he owned a small basketball team called the Cleveland Pipers. Steinbrenner led the entire franchise into bankruptcy.

That stretch of failure seemed to follow Steinbrenner when he took over the Yankees in the 1970s, as the team struggled with a number of setbacks and losses throughout the 1980s and 1990s. However, despite public outcry and criticism of Steinbrenner's controversial decisions, he led the team to an amazing comeback with six World Series entries between 1996 and 2003, and another championship in 2009. Today the Yankees are one of the most profitable teams in Major League Baseball.

Arianna Huffington is now one of the most recognizable names in media, but she was once rejected by three dozen major publishers. In 2009, Huffington was named as number 12 in *Forbes* Magazine's first-ever list of the "Most Influential Women In Media." In 2011, AOL acquired *The Huffington Post* for $315 million and made Huffington President and Editor-in-Chief of The Huffington Post Media Group, which included *The Huffington Post* and then-existing AOL properties such as AOL Music, Engadget, Patch Media, and StyleList. *Forbes* currently lists her as one of the most powerful women in the world. You think she is happy she did not give up on her dreams after her 35th rejection?

We want you to draw inspiration from these stories the next time you experience a setback or failure. At the time, some failures and setbacks can seem like the end of the road; but remember, there are countless successful men and women in the world today who are only enjoying success because they decided to push past the temporary moment of failure.

Learn from your mistakes, reflect and accept the failure, but stay true to your passion and keep pursuing your goals.

The Top 30 Things to do to Become a *Resale Millionaire*

There is a popular time travel movie trilogy in which the villain—now an old man—goes back in time to when he was in high school. He takes with him a book of sports trivia, which he gives to his younger self. The younger version of him then uses the book to become obscenely rich by betting on sporting events, knowing full well in advance who would win every single time. And thus history is forever altered.

Imagine this book as your time machine—you can go ahead into the future right this moment. You can travel to a time when you have built a multimillion-dollar business, and you talk to the much older and wiser version of you. What hard won knowledge would future-millionaire-you tell present-day-you?

Here are 30 insights that future *Resale Millionaires* would want you to know:

1. **Get clear on what you want and WHY you want it.** Sure, a goal of $5,000 a month or $25,000 a month is great, but what's your reason for wanting it? Obviously it's not because you love pieces of paper with dead presidents. It's because of what the money can DO for you. So WHY do you want a successful business? To get out of the dead end job you are stuck in? To spend time with your family? To retire on your favorite island? Once you are clear on your vision, it's a lot easier to take the steps necessary to achieve your dreams.

2. **You are smarter than you think.** Maybe you've been conned into thinking you need just "one more" tool or secret piece of information before you can get started—and that was about 4 dozen books or seminars ago. Odds are you already know more than enough to get started, and you can learn the rest as you go. So if you haven't already, stop stalling and take action!

3. **Motivation comes from within.** Waiting to work on your business "when you feel like it" means one thing: Failure. No one has ever built anything worthwhile by only working on things when they "felt" like it. Some days you have to bite the bullet, roll up your sleeves, and just get on with it. And if that

means canceling your cable subscription or having someone slap you every time you get distracted or procrastinate—do it. It's worth it.

4. **Speaking of getting distracted—STOP IT.** Make a plan and work the plan. Find your big picture and only do the things that will get you there. For example, if your goal is to build the best widget website ever, then don't get distracted by how much money is being made by others. Otherwise, you should have as much interest in other opportunities as you do in the life of a cow-dung eating bacteria. Seriously. I don't know how else to say this—FOCUS!!! Absolutely, positively nothing great was ever created without focus and yes, hard work. So bite the damn bullet and JUST DO IT. (You can't tell us that future-self wouldn't be giving present-self some tough love. You KNOW you need it.)

5. **The magic button that creates money out of thin air? Does not exist.** So stop chasing it, and stop believing it, and stop blowing your hard earned money on it. Success takes work. Making money takes work. Yes, business can be pretty simple and straight forward, but THERE IS NO PUSH BUTTON MAGIC MONEY SYSTEM. If there was, do you really think they would be selling it for $97?

6. **There's nothing noble about doing things the hard way.** Automating everything possible in your business is essential to getting the most out of your business. Anything that can be automated should be automated, as quickly as possible. If you can't automate it, see if you can outsource it. Outsource every tedious thing you do so you can focus on working on your business instead of in your business.

7. **Step back.** You're making progress, but are you headed in the right direction? Every week take time out to examine

what's happening in your business and if you're going in the right direction.

8. **Stop complaining.** Just. Stop. Do you know how much money you make when you whine, moan, groan and complain? Zip. Ziltch. Nada. So knock that crap off.

9. **Don't worry about your competition.** Know why? Because the vast majority of your competition is mediocre, and you don't stop until you reach great. Don't put out a product or service you wouldn't be proud to show to every single one of your colleagues. When you only produce great things, you have already passed 90% of your competition. The other 10% are the people you should get to know and associate with.

10. **Never stop learning.** While you know enough to get started building your business right now, you don't know enough to sustain it for the next 10 years. That's why you must always be learning more about your market niche and more about the marketing methods that apply to your business.

11. **Face your fears head on.** If you let fear rule your life, you'll never accomplish anything new and you'll never experience anything exciting. Fear is simply that funny feeling you get just before you're about to stretch yourself or do something new. Embrace fear—it's the signpost that says you're headed for greater things.

12. **Making money is simple.** You take certain steps, you get certain results. But it takes work, which is why it isn't easy and why not everyone is doing it. Just about anyone could do it, but most people simply are not willing to pay the price.

13. **Smart, successful people have goals.** If you don't write down your goals, you're just playing at building a business, and not actually doing it. A successful, profitable business has goals and business plans. Where's yours? BTW, writing down your goals

is the surest way not to feel overwhelmed and out of control. Feeling anxiety? Afraid you can't achieve something you want? Write it down and then formulate a plan to get it—in writing.

14. **Never compromise your character or your good name.** Anything placed on the Internet stays out there forever. Want to call someone a bad name online? DON'T do it. Thinking of promoting a crap product that's making money like gangbusters? DON'T do it. Being a person of integrity will bring you more customers, more success, and more wealth in the long run, regardless of the missed opportunities for a quick buck. So always act with the highest regard for your fellow man and woman.

15. **Be you.** Often people try to wear a persona when they begin their new business. If you do this, you'll have to continue to wear that persona forever—unless you kill your persona off, in which case you'll have to start all over again. Instead, why not simply be that one of a kind creation you already are? Yourself. You have far more to offer others than you realize. You simply have to figure out what those things are and then use them to be the best you that you can be.

16. **If you already have 2-3 excellent ideas on how to make money, you likely have enough information to make 6 figures a year.** No joke. We're going to figure you don't care for one of the methods, but you're fully capable of implementing at least one of the other two. There are literally thousands of people who have already proven this is true—you only need one solid workable system to make real money in business. So stop cruising through life and get busy. Now!

17. **Be warned: Others might not understand what you're doing.** They might even resent it. They might try to hold you back. They might discourage you. They might be a total energy drain.

And they might do everything in their power to stop you. Their motivation? Many and varied, but the bottom line is that your new business is perceived as a threat to them. If they're family, explain that you need to do this and you are not changing your mind. If they are friends, consider placing some distance between yourself and them. You can catch up with them later once your business is rocking—at which time you might be surprised to find out you need new friends because your old ones resent your success. Sad but true.

18. **What you do today will predict what you become tomorrow.** Are you diligently moving forward? Or are you putting things off? Choose your habits wisely. I wish I could imprint that on your hand so you would see it every day. ***Choose. Your. Habits. Wisely.***

19. **Stop focusing on the economy or the politicians and just get busy.** We know people who spend their days watching economic news and then lament that it's impossible right now to successfully start a business. And I know others who ignore that same news and make news of their own, starting tremendously successful businesses in the weakest of economies. Remember, whatever you focus on gets bigger.

20. **It's all about selling. Period.** You're either selling a product, a service, or something else, but you are in fact selling. If you are not selling, you are not making money. Focus 90% of your time on the sales process.

21. **Content rules.** Social networks, applications, software, etc. will come and go, but content has always and will always work because people will always demand high quality content, regardless of format.

22. **Build your own tribe.** Pick your corner of the Internet, whatever that might be (call it a niche if you like), and then

build a solid and ever-growing tribe of people who know you and trust you as THE GUY or GAL in that niche. Don't worry about those that don't fit your tribe—just focus on those who do and you will always have an income.

23. **Don't buy "stuff" with your profits.** That new TV and new car can wait another year or two. Right now, invest all of your profits back into your business. This is how people retire in just 5 to 15 years, by reinvesting now to scale up their businesses. Work the numbers. If you're investing $1 that yields $2, then you are effectively doubling your money over and over again. If you instead invest that money in a new car, the money and it's future earning potential is forever lost to you.

24. **Use deadlines.** This is your business, not a hobby, so treat it like a business. Think strategically about what needs to be done and write it down, complete with deadlines. Then do everything in your power to meet those deadlines, no matter what.

25. **In the beginning, do not take a day off.** Focus on your goals daily or they will fall by the wayside. Missing even one day can lead to missing two days, which can lead to missing a week, which leads to a month lost. Everyday re-read your goals and do at least one thing that takes you closer to reaching your larger goals, even if it only takes 20 minutes. It's not about how much time you put in, it's about how much you get done with the time you have, and how consistently you make progress.

26. **Forgo all distractions.** Hobbies, television, video games, vacations, etc., are all things you can put off for at least your first 4 to 8 months. Set a goal of what you're going to accomplish by a 6-month deadline, and only when you accomplish it can you afford to be distracted. Yes, you've got to get serious about your business—enough fooling around; it's time to actually make it happen.

27. **Find a mentor. Or a coach.** If you want to accomplish a whole lot more in a whole lot less time, with fewer mistakes along the way, find someone who's already doing what you want to do and hang onto their coattails for dear life until you can do it on your own. Yes, coaches cost money in the short run, but in the long run it's one of the best investments you'll ever make.

28. **Figure it will take 3-5 years to build any real wealth.** Look back at where you were 5 years ago and imagine if you had started your business then; think about where you would be today. Now look ahead 5 years and realize it all begins now.

29. **Build a support team.** This might simply be a group of 3 to 6 people who get together in person or via Skype to brainstorm and report progress. Nothing beats having fresh minds looking at your business, or the moral support of being in the company of others going through the same process you're living. And if possible, get a couple of experienced businesses and marketers to join your group and act as mentors.

30. **This one is for the long haul: Have an exit strategy.** There may come a day when you want to sell your business, either to start a new one or to retire. By planning for this in advance, you might be able to sell your business for more. For example, be sure to actively build individual lists of prospects, buyers and associates because not only will these make you money, they're also tremendous assets when you sell.

And remember to give your business a name and brand of its own. If you name it after yourself, it will be difficult to sell unless you find another person who shares your name. You will need to do everything possible to solely own that name. Purchase all of the domain extensions available and any variations, along with getting all applicable copyrights and trademarks.

Something to think about: Research shows that 80% of penta-millionaires (those with a net worth of $5 million or more) are entrepreneurs who sold their businesses.[38]

Imagine you're standing on a timeline at the exact juncture where it branches in two different directions. One direction takes you to that million-dollar business, and the other direction has you spending the rest of your life just as it is now, with no changes and no big success.

You choose which path to take. The million-dollar-future-you is waiting to guide you to that destiny—if you choose. Or you can do nothing, and the other destiny will happen pretty much on its own. It's your choice.

That's it—your head is full and it's time for you to go back and get busy on your business, keeping in mind everything future you said.

Closing the Garage Door

Tony Robbins is fond of saying that "Success leaves clues," and he's right. Now it's time to choose your method of attaining your goal, and then reverse engineer your way to success.

So let's say your goal is to make $10,000 a month with an online business, since that's a very popular goal among new entrepreneurs.

How do you want to make that income? Perhaps you want to create and sell products in a particular niche, or list build, or build a membership site. Your first step is to decide what it is that you want to do and what niche you want to do it in.

If you've got your niche selected but you don't know what to do next, then your first step is to find every big marketer in that niche and get on his or her lists. See what they're doing, what they're saying, and especially what they're selling. This should give you some terrific ideas in less than a week's time. Write down all of your ideas, even the ones you think are silly or beyond your reach.

Then, narrow your choices. Maybe you've decided to create a blog, build a list and sell affiliate products and your own membership site. Now you have a plan. You can get basic info from the Internet on starting your blog and list building to get you started.

Next, you're going to analyze what your competitors are doing that's working in terms of blogging, list building, selling affiliate products, and running a membership site in your niche. It's been said that if you want to know the real secrets of what the best online business marketers do, then you should watch what they do rather than listen to what they say. That's why you joined your competitors' lists—to see how they're doing and what they're doing.

Questions to research: How are they getting traffic? Where do they get their link?

Who are their affiliates? What is their content strategy? What is their unique selling point? How do they structure their websites? Who is their audience? What is their website or product missing? And so on.

But, you've never done it before? You're nervous? You're shy? You've got butterflies in your stomach and you feel like you're going to throw up? Congratulations! You're about to do something that is going to stretch your abilities and get you one step closer to realizing your dream, so thumb your nose at fear and do it anyway.

Opening Up Shop

Our journey to becoming *Resale Millionaires* started with a cancer diagnosis, and a welcome distraction in exploring the treasure troves of estate sales. What began as a hobby led to a full-scale, family run small business. But it wasn't just profit that we gained—it was a whole new appreciation for life. Our tragedy showed us the importance of creating the life we desired and pushed us to live life to the fullest. Our fulfillment and love produced this book, which was written with the goal of enhancing both your life and your livelihood.

We have taken all that we have learned over the years and compiled those lessons into these pages. We have provided you with a blueprint for your business that instructs you on where to go, what to buy, and how to resell for a profit. We know from experience that building a small business isn't easy—a lot of the advice in this book was learned the hard way. Luckily you can learn from our mistakes and successes, and use this book to help you along the way to becoming a *Resale Millionaire*.

We believe that first and foremost you need to determine what will make you happy. What is your passion and purpose—the "why" behind creating your business? From there you can decide how to specialize and align your business with your life vision. We have provided a myriad of questions to answer, tips to follow, and suggestions to implement. You have read success stories, and cautionary tales of failed business models. You understand the importance of being IN business, and you possess the knowledge and tools to make the most of doing business on the Internet. You learned how to avoid common pitfalls, determine CSFs, and strategize your marketing plan by incorporating social media. You know how to manage your time and resources to create a successful business that will help you achieve overall fulfillment and satisfaction.

In short, you know how to live life as a *Resale Millionaire*. We hope you enjoy it as much as we do.

AFTERWORD

If our story and business approach has resonated with you and you want to follow in our footsteps, we can help coach and mentor you along the way. You don't have to do it alone. Want success faster? Want to leverage the tools and training we took years to develop? Want to learn more? Just visit www.ResaleMillionaires.com and get started on creating your success today!

We thank you for investing your time and money in this book, and wish you all the best! If you have any questions or feedback, just send us a message and we will do our best to answer it.

Karen & Dennis Stemmle

Appendix A
CHECKLIST FOR STARTING YOUR BUSINESS

While every business is different and no checklist can account for all the variables you will encounter, we wanted to provide you with a starting point of questions and ideas to help you improve your overall chances of business success.

Deciding on a Business

- Have you considered starting part-time without quitting your job?
- Have you objectively compared your selection with a number of other business possibilities?
- Have you prepared a "for" and "against" list to clarify your thinking?
- Have you worked for someone else in your intended business to get a true feel for the day to day?

- Is your intended business something you will enjoy doing that is aligned with your vision?
- Have you test marketed your product or service to gain feedback?
- Have you reviewed the advantages and disadvantages of starting with a partner?
- Have you talked to successful people in your intended business?
- Have you prepared a one-year cash flow projection?
- If starting part-time, will your business conflict with your job?
- Have you set a limit on how much you can risk?
- Have you written a business plan?
- Have you checked your zoning ordinance?

Financing the Business

- Have you saved enough money to start your business?
- Are you willing to start small to minimize the capital required?
- Do you have financing in place to support your cash flow projection?
- Have you investigated the S.B.A. loan guarantee program?
- Have you looked to suppliers as sources of financing?
- Have you considered bartering as a source of financing?
- Are you prepared to live frugally to keep your living costs at a minimum?
- Do your cash flow projections bring you to break even?

Your Business Name

- Is the name you selected appropriate for the business, easy to remember, easy to spell, and does it create a visual image?
- Is the .com version of your name available? If not, seriously consider finding a name where you can obtain a matching URL.

- Have you trademarked your business name?

Business Organization

- Have you had the assistance of your lawyer and accountant in deciding what type of organization is best for you?
- Do you need a pension plan in place?
- Where will you get health insurance?
- If you have a partner, do you have a written buy-sell agreement in place?
- Have you joined a local Chamber of Commerce?
- Do you have a logo?
- Have you secured stationary, business cards, and business forms?
- Who will build your website?
- Have you secured all your social media account names?

Licenses and Permits

- All businesses require licenses and/or permits from the City, County, State and/or Federal Government. Do you have yours?
- Is your location zoned for your business?
- Is your home approved for a home-based business?
- Do you have the Certificate of Occupancy if leasing space?
- Do you need a Seller's Permit (also called a Certificate of Resale) to allow you to collect sales tax on your merchandise?
- Do you have an Employer Identification Number (EIN)?

Insurance

- Check with an insurance agent for the coverage you will need for your type of business. Typical coverage may include:
  - Business property insurance
  - Liability

- ◆ Worker's Compensation
- ◆ Fire
- ◆ Medical
- ◆ Life
- ◆ Flood or Earthquake
- ◆ Errors and Omissions

Communication Tools

- Email service
- Voice over IP Phone Service (VOIP)
- Fax line with dedicated phone number
- Computers including back-up equipment (external hard drive and DVD)
- Mobile communications equipment including laptop, notebook, or smartphone.
- Contact Management Solution (CMA)

Commerce

- Is a Point of Sale Systems required and in place?
- Are Merchant accounts set up to accept payments?
- Are websites and blogs ready to process payments?

Location and Leasing

- Have you secured a location for your business?
- Have you asked for a short-term lease with options to renew?
- Has your lawyer reviewed your lease?

Accounting and Cash Flow

- Is your accounting software in place?
- Are you prepared to reconcile your bank account every month?

- Are you planning to keep your own records or outsource book keeping?
- Have you set up an account with a payroll service provider to handle state and federal payroll returns?
- Have you set up a business account at your bank?
- Do you know the tax liability issues? (Income tax, Quarterly returns, Payroll tax)
- Do you have safeguards against employee theft?

Opening and Marketing

- Are all your signs installed?
- Are all licenses, permits and certificate of occupancy secured?
- Is your merchandise displayed attractively?
- Is the advertising and promotional material secured?
- Have you started developing a mailing list database?
- Do you know how and where your successful competitors advertise and market their products or services?
- Have you joined trade associations?
- Are you clear in your messaging about the benefits your business products or services provide?

Managing Employees

- Does your HR policy include job descriptions, hourly rates, incentives, and holidays?
- Do you have policies and procedures to ensure compliance with federal and state laws?
- Are you displaying all the signs and posters that may be required by law for your business?
- Do your employees project a pleasant and positive image?
- Do your employees like people and relate well to them?

- Are your employees helpful to customers as well as to other team members?
- Are your employees completely trained?
- Do your employees know the product, merchandise, or the service provided inside and out?
- Have you established a work schedule and hours of operation?

This checklist is in no way comprehensive, but it will provide you with questions and ideas to get you started. Please feel free to add or subtract your own questions and ideas to better fit your business.

Appendix B
IDEAS FOR ITEMS YOU CAN BUY AND RESELL

Advertising

- Matchbooks
- Matchboxes
- Premiums—promotional items like toys, collectibles, souvenirs and household products that are linked to a product, and often require box tops, tokens or proofs of purchase to acquire.
- Radio premiums
- Prizes
- Bazooka Joe comics from Bazooka bubble gum
- Cereal box prizes
- Cracker Jack prizes
- Pin-back buttons
- Tazos from Frito Lay products
- Brand name products
- Avon
- Campbell's Soup
- Coca-Cola
- Disneyana

- Disney pin trading
- Harley Davidson
- John Deere

- Maytag
- Ronson's Lighters
- Zippo lighters

Architectural

- Fireplace
- Furniture
- Hardware

- Lighting, lamps, lampshades
- Locks and keys
- Tile

Art & Photography

- Valuable works of art
- Artifacts
- Folk Art

- Native American art
- Photographs
- Prints

Books, Magazines, and Paper

- Absolut vodka ads
- Got Milk? ads
- Vintage ads
- Autographs
- Map collecting

- Globes
- Roadmaps
- Paperweights
- Sticker (paper)

Books & Periodicals

- Books
- Children's literature
- First editions
- Comic books

- Manga
- Magazines
- Magazine clippings
- Newspapers

Cards

- Artist trading cards
- Phone-cards

- Playing cards
- Jokers

- Tarot cards
- Postcards
- Trade cards
- Cigarette cards
- Tea cards
- Trading cards
- Magic cards
- Insert cards

- Non-sports cards
- Sports cards
- Baseball cards
- Basketball cards
- Football cards
- Hockey cards
- Jersey cards

Ephemera

Ephemera is transitory written and printed matter not intended to be retained or preserved. Some collectable ephemera is listed below:

- Air sickness bags
- Bookmarks
- Brochures and Guide books
- Cheese labels
- Greeting cards
- Lottery tickets
- Movie tickets
- Newsletters
- Passports

- Pamphlets
- Postcards
- Posters
- Public transport timetables
- Airline timetables
- Railroad timetables
- Sugar sachets
- Tea bag labels
- Tea bag wrappers
- Tickets

Clothing, Fabric, Textiles

- Fashion portal
- Knitting portal
- Buttons
- Needlework
- Quilts

- Scutelliphily (patches and badges)
- Sewing
- Textiles
- Thimbles

- Vintage clothing and accessories

Coins, Currency, Stamps

- Numismatics
- Coin collecting
- Notaphily (Paper currency)
- Exonumia (numismatic items such as tokens and medals)
- Token coins
- Scripophily
- Bonds
- Stocks
- Philately (stamps and postal history)
- Federal duck stamps
- First day covers
- Postmarks
- Stamp collecting

Film and Television

- DVDs
- Films
- Film props
- Movie posters
- Television shows
- Videocassette tapes

Glass and Pottery

- Bakeware and cookware
- China, porcelain, and pottery
- Art pottery
- Nippon porcelain
- Whisky decanters
- Jim Beam bottles
- Glass and crystal
- Art glass
- Bread plates
- Bottles
- Beer bottles
- Milk bottles
- Perfume bottles
- Snuff bottles
- Wine bottles
- Depression glass
- Insulator (electrical)
- Paperweights
- Pattern glass
- Shot glass

Household

- Appliances
- Beverage coasters
- Candles
- Corks
- Figurines
- Netsuke (miniature Japanese sculptures)
- Holiday collectibles
- Jewelry and gemstones
- Keyrings
- Music boxes
- Perfume bottles
- Sterling silver
- Utensils and silverware

Kitchen Collectibles

- Bottle caps
- Beverage cans
- Beverage can tabs
- Cast iron cookware
- Cookie cutters
- Cookie jars
- Hip flasks
- Housewares
- Lunch boxes
- Mason jars
- Refrigerator magnets
- Shakers: salt, pepper, sugar
- Tea bags
- Teapots

Memorabilia

Memorabilia includes collectables related to a person, organization, event or media.

Event Memorabilia

- Sports memorabilia
- Baseballs and baseball bats
- Boxing fight programs and posters
- World's Fair

Media Memorabilia

- Film memorabilia
- Film props
- Movie posters

Organization Memorabilia

- Police memorabilia
- Political memorabilia
- Bumper stickers
- Campaign buttons
- Scouting memorabilia
- Military
- University
- Corporate

Music

- Records
- CDs
- Jukeboxes
- Cassette tapes
- Musical instruments
- Analog synthesizers
- Tube amplifiers
- Vintage guitars

Nature and Animals

- Butterfly collecting
- Conchology (collecting seashells)
- Crystals
- Fossil collecting
- Mineral collecting
- Gemstones
- Insects
- Oology (collecting eggs)
- Plants
- Rocks
- Skulls and Skeletons

Sports (Professional & Collegiate)

- Apparel
- Cards
- Equipment
- Gear
- Jewelry
- Pennants

Technology

- Automobilia
- Bicycles
- Calculators
- Clocks and watches
- Computers (especially Vintage computers)
- Fans (Vintage/Collectible)
- Firearms
- Fireworks

- Fountain pens
- Jukeboxes
- Knives
- Motorcycles
- Phonographs
- Photographica
- Cameras
- Movie cameras and projectors
- Radios
- Record players
- Recording media (see Film and television, Music)
- Scales
- Scientific instruments
- Telephones
- Televisions
- Tools
- Hand tools
- Tractors
- Vending machines (coin-operated machines)
- Weapons
- Writing Implements
- Inkwells

Theme

A theme collection includes related or unrelated items that have a unifying theme or common thread, or a collection that fits the scope of a special interest.

General Themes

- Airline
- Animals: amphibians, birds, cats, dogs, fish, horses, invertebrates, pigs, reptiles, etc.
- Automotive
- Automobiles
- Classic cars
- Vintage cars
- License plates
- Oil cans
- Farming
- Gambling/gaming
- Casino chip collecting
- Hawaiiana
- Orientalia
- Space

Historical Themes

- Breweriana
- Beer can
- Militaria
- American Civil War
- Phaleristics (orders, medals, decorations)
- Military art
- Military models
- Military uniforms
- Model figures
- Tin soldiers
- Petroliana
- Railroad
- Science fiction
- Tobacciana
- Cigar boxes
- Cigar cases
- Cigarette cases
- Cigarette holders
- Lighters
- Smoking pipes
- Western Americana
- Cowboy

Travel Themes

- Souvenirs
- Post Cards
- Souvenir spoons
- Trunks

Toys, Games, Dolls

- Action figures
- Board games
- Collectible card games
- Dolls
- Barbie dolls
- Beanie babies
- Blythe dolls
- Porcelain Dolls
- Raggedy Ann & Andy dolls
- Teddy bears
- Toy soldiers
- Figurines
- Keshi erasers
- Marbles
- Mechanical banks
- Model cars
- Corgi
- Hot Wheels
- Matchbox
- Webkinz
- Model horses
- Breyer
- Pez

- Piggy banks
- Playing Cards
- Pogs
- Rubber duck
- Scale models
- Model airplanes
- Dyna Flites
- Herpa Wings

- Schabak (German die-cast airplanes)
- Matchbox Skybusters
- Model trains
- Ship models
- GUNPLA (plastic model kits)
- Video games and equipment

Fitness

- Equipment
- DVD Programs
- Yoga

- Clothing
- Gear

REFERENCES

1   Clark, T. *The Biggest Myth About Family Businesses*. 2014.
    Forbes. Retrieved June 2014: (http://www.forbes.com/sites/
    groupthink/2014/05/20/the-biggest-myth-about-family-business/)

2   Astrachan, J. H. and Shanker, M. C. (2003), *Family Businesses'
    Contribution to the U.S. Economy: A Closer Look. Family Business
    Review*, 16: 211-219. Retrieved November 2012: (http://
    onlinelibrary.wiley.com/doi/10.1111/j.1741-6248.2003.
    tb00015.x/abstract.)

3   Zellweger, Nason, Nordqvist. From *Longevity of Firms to
    Transgenerational Entrepreneurship of Families: Introducing Family
    Entrepreneurial Orientation*. Retrieved November 2012: (http://c.
    ymcdn.com/sites/www.ffi.org/resource/resmgr/docs/goodman_
    study.pdf.)

4   Zellweger, Nason, Nordqvist. *From Longevity of Firms to
    Transgenerational Entrepreneurship of Families: Introducing Family
    Entrepreneurial Orientation*. Retrieved November 2012: (http://c.
    ymcdn.com/sites/www.ffi.org/resource/resmgr/docs/goodman_
    study.pdf.)

5   US Department of Commerce, Bureau of the Census. *Statistics for All U.S. Firms That Were Family-Owned by Industry, Gender, Ethnicity, Race, and Veteran Status for the U.S.: 2007 Survey of Business Owners.* Retrieved November 2012: (http:// factfinder2.census.gov/faces/tableservices/jsf/pages/productview. xhtml?pid=SBO200700CSCB04&prodType=table)

6   *Family Business Alliance.* Retrieved June 2014:(http:// www.fbagr.org/index.php?option=com_ content&view=article&id=117&Itemid=75)

7   *Family Business Alliance.* Retrieved June 2014: (http://www.fbagr.org/index.php?option=com_ content&view=article&id=117&Itemid=75)

8   Deutesche Bank Group. *Wealth with Responsibility Study/2000.* Retrieved November 2012: (http://www.bc.edu/content/dam/files/ research_sites/cwp/pdf/wwr.pdf)

9   *Greater Washington D.C. Family Business Alliance. Family Business Fun Facts.* Retrieved November 2012: (http://www. dcfamilybusiness.com/resources/knowledge-base/family-business-fun-facts)

10 Walmart 2012 Annual Report. Retrieved December 2012: (*http:// www.walmartstores.com/sites/annual-report/2012/WalMart_AR.pdf*)

11 Anderson, R. C. and Reeb, D. M. (2003), Founding-Family Ownership and Firm Performance: Evidence from the S&P 500. The Journal of Finance. Retrieved November 2012: (*http:// onlinelibrary.wiley.com/doi/10.1111/1540-6261.00567/abstract*)

12 Mass Mutual American Family Business Survey, 2007. Retrieved November 2012: http://www.massmutual.com/mmfg/pdf/afbs. pdf.)14 (University of New Hampshire Center for Family Business. Family Business Facts. Retrieved November 2012: (http://www. familybusiness.unh.edu/usefulinfo/FamilyBusinessFacts.pdf)

13 Mass Mutual American Family Business Survey, 2007. Retrieved November 2012: (http://www.massmutual.com/mmfg/pdf/afbs.pdf.)

14 Mass Mutual American Family Business Survey, 2007. Retrieved November 2012: (http://www.massmutual.com/mmfg/pdf/afbs.pdf.)

15 Peak Family Business Survey. 2011. Retrieved June 2014: (http://www.amserv.com/index.cfm/page/Family-Business-Statistics/pid/10715.html)

16 Manfred Zimmermann, "Neurophysiology of Sensory Systems," in *Fundamentals of Sensory Physiology*, 3rd, rev. ed. Robert F. Schmidt (New York: Springer, 1986), 116.

17 J.W. Schooler and T.Y. Engstler-Schooler, "Verbal Overshadowing of Visual Memories: Some Things Are Better Left Unsaid," Cognitive Psychology 22: 36-71 (1990).

18 Owens, Ryan; Scholz, Jim (March 20, 2012). *Redneck' Millionaires Built "Duck Dynasty" in Duck Call Business. ABC News*. Retrieved April 8, 2012.

19 Zoppe Family Website: http://zoppe.net/page4.html

20 The Sustainable Development Solutions Network September 2013 http://unsdsn.org/resources/publications/world-happiness-report-2013/

21 Grossman, Lev, Lacayo, Richard (16 October 2005). *All-Time 100 Novels: The Complete List*. Time.

22 Phil Robertson, *Happy, Happy, Happy*, Howard Books (2013) P. 110-111

23 When less is more: Counterfactual thinking and satisfaction among Olympic medalists.v Medvec, Victoria Husted; Madey, Scott F.; Gilovich, Thomas Journal of Personality and Social Psychology, Vol 69(4), Oct 1995, 603-610. http://dx.doi.org/10.1037/0022-3514.69.4.603

24 http://www.npr.org/blogs/thetorch/2012/08/03/157835076/would-you-rather-win-silver-or-bronze-be-careful-what-you-wish-for

25 http://darrenhardy.success.com/2010/10/not-about-what-you-do/

26 https://www.google.com/?gws_rd=ssl#q=average+price+of+home+in+silicon+valley

27 https://www.google.com/?gws_rd=ssl#q=google+foundersy+net+worth

28 *Blockbuster Reaches Agreement on Plan to Recapitalize Balance Sheet and Substantially Reduce its Indebtedness.* (Press release). Blockbuster. September 23, 2010. Retrieved 2010-09-23.

29 Fritz, Ben (April 7, 2011). "Dish Network wins bidding for assets of bankrupt Blockbuster". *Los Angeles Times.* Retrieved 2011-05-02.

30 http://en.wikipedia.org/wiki/Ross_Perot

31 Liker, J. 2004. *The Toyota Way: 14 Management Principles from the World's Greatest Manufacturer.*

32 http://www.ehow.com/how-does_5212542_many-businesses-fail-first-year_.html

33 http://en.wikipedia.org/wiki/Drop_shipping - cite_note-4

34 http://en.wikipedia.org/wiki/Amazon.com - cite_note-byers-7

35 http://www.cultivate-communications.com/2014/02/3-seconds-get-attention/

36 http://blog.wishpond.com/post/55782776914/pinterest-seo-a-guide-for-businesses

37 http://www.socialmediatoday.com/content/second-largest-search-engine-infographic

38 https://www.growthink.com/exit-strategy